W9-BKA-214

The Unknown Island

The Unk

Ian Smith / Douglas & McIntyre Ltd.

nown Island

LIBRARY
LINCOLN MEMORIAL UNIVERSITY
Harrogate Tennessee 37752

113465

QH 106.2
B8
S58

Text and colour photographs copyright © Ian Smith, 1973
Black and white photographs copyright © Robert Keziere, 1973

All rights reserved. No part of this book may be reproduced or transmitted
in any form by any means without permission in writing from the publisher,
except by a reviewer, who may quote brief passages in a review.

Douglas & McIntyre Ltd.
1615 Venables Street
Vancouver, British Columbia

Canadian Cataloguing in Publication Data

Smith, Ian, 1939-1977

  The Unknown Island

  ISBN 0-88894-033-5

  1. Natural History — British Columbia — Vancouver Island. I. Title.
QH106.2.B8S58   574.9711'34   C82-091065-1

Black and white photographs with the exception of those appearing
on pages 63, 65, 124, 126, 141, 143 ("wave patterns in the sand at
Pachena Bay") and 170 by Robert Keziere.
Drawings by Carl Chaplin.
Map courtesy of the Survey and Mapping Branch, Department of
Energy, Mines and Resources, with detail work by Doris Stastny.
Design by Jim Rimmer.
Typography by Vancouver Typesetting Co. Ltd.
Printed and bound in Canada by Evergreen Press Limited, Vancouver.

ACKNOWLEDGEMENTS

A great many people have offered help and encouragement during the completion of this book, but I am particularly indebted to the following individuals all of whom reviewed portions of the original manuscript and improved it substantially with their suggestions: Ed Barraclough, Pete Beyer, Chris Brayshaw, Dave Jensen, Peter Macnair, Byron Mason, George Reid, Adam Szczawinski and Bob Tustin.

For Vandy and Dana

CONTENTS

Triangle I.

Scott   Islands

QUEEN

Cape Sutil
Shuttleworth Bight   Bull
Nissen Bight   Harbour
Nels Bight
Cape Scott

CHARLOTTE

PORT
HARDY

Hansen Lagoon

Holberg

Holberg Inlet

Coal
Harbour

SOUND

ALERT
BAY

PORT
McNEILL

JOHNSTONE

Winter
Harbour

QUATSINO
SOUND

PORT
ALICE

VANCOUVER

Nimpkish L.

Bonanza Range

Tsitika

Claud
Elliott
L.

Lawn Point

Brooks
Peninsula

Johnson
Lagoon

Schoen L.

Cape Cook

Bunsby
Islands

Kyoquot

Tahsish
Inlet   Artlish

Fair Harbour

Woss L.

Kyoquot
Sound

ZEBALLOS

Rugged
Mountain

TAHSIS

Tlupana

NOOTKA

Tlupana

Tlupana
Inlet

ISLAND

Nootka

Mucha

Friendly Cove

PACIFIC

NOOTKA

SOUND

Hesquiat
Peninsula

Hot Sprin
Cove

Estevan Point

OCEAN

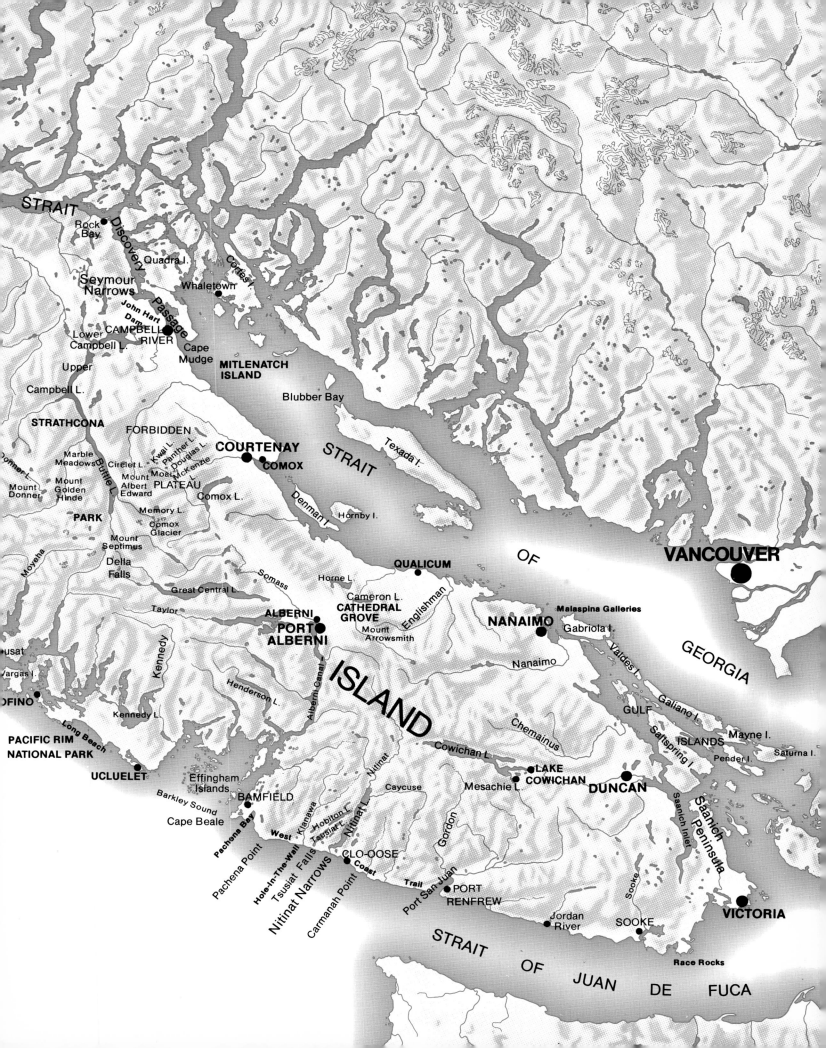

A Land of Many Faces

Vancouver Island has a way of surprising people. They are surprised by its size (almost the length of Ireland), its beauty, its incredible diversity and even its shape on the map. But few people have the opportunity to discover even a portion of what the island has to offer.

Unless they live nearby, people usually hear of Vancouver Island only by accident. It rates a place in geography texts as the most southwesterly part of Canada and a place in history books because Captain Cook chose to come ashore at a village called Nootka during his search for the northwest passage. And it makes the news every so often because sea captains persist in steering their freighters onto its west coast reefs.

Visitors to the island of course discover more: the curious arbutus trees which shed their bark instead of their leaves; the magnificent Garry oaks, mute testimony to a fine climate rivalling that of California; the beautiful domestic gardens which reflect not only the mild climate but also the general inclinations of the populace; the gentle beaches crowded only near the cities; the fields of strawberries and corn and potatoes (fewer each year as the sub-divisions grow); and the cities themselves, small and haphazardly laid out, but the residents like it that way.

The island's east coast is the most hospitable in climate, and the easiest to reach. Few people ever get beyond it, confining their view of the island to an area close to the narrow strip of highway running north from Victoria, its largest city, to Kelsey Bay, a dot at the end of the blacktop.

Some take a side trip to Port Alberni because it lies on the route to Pacific Rim National Park and for years, people found real adventure by braving a steep and dusty logging road to reach the grandeur of the surf at Long Beach. They came despite uncommon hardships, suffering blowouts and broken axles and overheated engines, leaving mufflers and tail pipes and even entire cars strewn along the route. Or else they hitch-hiked, sprawling forlornly by the roadside in sun and rain, sometimes ten and twenty in line, caked in dust or mud and dodging flying gravel, but considering it worth the trouble to walk the sand barefoot and listen to the waves at night.

All that is over now, for the one constant fact of Vancouver Island is change. A new road to Long Beach eliminates the frightening switchbacks which ruined so many cars, but it eliminates much of the adventure too, and it is bringing more people. Those who saw the beach in the early days, twelve miles of sand and often no man-made tracks except their own, ask where the "progress" will end. Perhaps it never will.

But Vancouver Island is far more than the east coast and Long Beach, and sometimes people read the names on the map and wonder. Kyoquot. Triangle Island. Tlupana River. Forbidden Plateau. Estevan Point. Euclataws Cavern. Kashutl Inlet. Mount Golden Hinde. And a thousand more, each with a story.

Kyoquot is one of the oldest settlements on the Pacific coast, a Nootka Indian Village that still depends, as it always has, upon the sea that surrounds it. It lies in complete isolation on a tiny island off the northwest coast, as pretty a setting as could be imagined on a good day...but on that coast, the weather is often foul.

Triangle Island is a naturalist's paradise, a curious angular spot in the ocean some thirty miles off the northwest tip of Vancouver Island. It is little more than a grassy hummock riddled with the burrows of seabirds, but it provides the breeding grounds for perhaps half the sea lions of southern British Columbia. Ripped by winds that were on one occasion strong enough to blow down part of a light station, when it is not windy, it is foggy. But when the sun shines, it is a glorious place with eagles wheeling overhead and sea lions roaring and surf thrashing against the steep shores.

Tlupana River? Just another west coast watershed, perhaps lovelier than most, which will be logged before most people know it exists.

Forbidden Plateau has for years been a favourite hiking area for alpinists. One story has it that the name stems from Indian times. There is a legend telling of a tribe that took its women and children to the plateau to hide them before a battle, but after the battle they could not be found and the area came to be known as a forbidden place. It is forbidden no longer, however, for the lakes are stocked with fish and the mountain meadows are an invitation to hiking and the peaks would challenge any rock climber.

Estevan Point is not only a fascinating piece of geography — a large, boggy peninsula with a flat, fragmented rock shelf extending hundreds of yards offshore — but it also has a lighthouse which was the only spot in North America directly attacked by the Japanese during World War II.

One day early in the war, a submarine surfaced offshore and lobbed a few shells towards the station, inflicting no significant damage but causing a major panic among navy personnel in Victoria who were attending a fancy-dress ball that evening.

Euclataws Cavern is simply one of many caves, albeit a particularly elaborate one; Kashutl Inlet, just one of over two dozen fiords along the island's west coast; Mount Golden Hinde, only one of hundreds of peaks. It is just coincidence that this mountain, the highest of them all, lies near the geographical center of the island.

And so it goes, simply names on the map to many people but each a place with its own significance. A few of the names may become familiar through happenstance — a shipwreck, a mining discovery, or an article in a magazine — but most remain unknown.

For those who know them, the names are signposts to gnarled vegetation and puffin colonies and twenty-pound steelhead trout; to monstrous trees and roaring surf and the last of the whales; to ptarmigan and ospreys and rotting totem poles; to elk meadows and beaver dams and deer herds; to sea otters and trumpeter swans and 10,000 Canada geese; to a wilderness quickly disappearing but still there for those who wish to seek it out.

The names mark an unfamiliar land, an area larger than most people imagine but still seemingly too small for the surprise and diversity it contains — the unknown island.

Overleaf/Huge Douglas fir on a southeast slope

THE FORESTS

1/A Green and Pleasant Land

The variety of Vancouver Island is endless. There is the coast, with surf and sea-birds and a constant wind. There are the mountains, a world of rocks and glaciers that seem to reach out forever. There are lakes and rivers, waterfalls and islands, beaches and caves. But most of all there is the forest, the face that the island most often puts before the world.

The original Vancouver Island forest could be described only as magnificent. The first visitors to the island found trees that were perhaps the finest in Canada: great brooding conifers that stood tall against the years, trees that had lived through eleven centuries and were still growing. They were often twelve feet in diameter, with bark as thick as the entire trunk of a tree in other Canadian forests: giants 300 feet tall, long enough to stretch across six city lots if laid out on the ground; incredibly tall, yet dwarfed by the country in which they grew.

The trees shape the character of the land and from far away or to the inexperienced eye, the island's forests appear quite uniform. But this is an illusion: the trees reflect the island's geography, and the geography of Vancouver Island is anything but uniform.

The island appears oblong or oval at first glance, but it is easier to think of it as a flattened triangle, with the west coast between Cape Scott and Sooke forming the base, and the tiny settlement of Rock Bay (between Campbell River and Kelsey Bay) forming the apex.

The entire west coast region comes under the moderating influence of the Pacific Ocean, a phrase which inhabitants recognize as a euphemism for a tremendous amount of rain. The official record is 19 inches in a single day at a spot near Ucluelet, but you can always run into a logger or prospector who will tell you of a storm he once sat out that made 19 inches seem like a heavy dew.

Sulphur polyphore fungus, common in mature forests

The rain results from Pacific clouds running into the island's mountains which lie tight up to the ocean along most of the west coast. Those living between Campbell River and Sooke are the beneficiaries of all this rain since, having dropped up to 300 inches annually on parts of the western half of the island, the storms have proportionately less to deliver to the east. In the extreme southeast corner of the island, the drying trend becomes complete, and there are areas which in some years have received as little as seventeen inches of precipitation. This makes it almost desert country, and in fact some cactus does grow there.

The other side of the triangle has a mixed climate. It receives less rain, on the average, than the west coast, but no one would consider the weather of the northeast coast truly enjoyable. The southern half of this area lies in the path of arctic winds which howl down the long coastal inlets in mid-winter, while the northern half lies unhappily within the influence of the storms which sweep in off Queen Charlotte Sound on their way down from Alaska, bringing with them a wind which rarely lets up even in summer. The wind gets a clear sweep at this part of the island, since the country is less mountainous than the areas to the south. And while the northern part of Vancouver Island may receive less rain because of its lack of tall mountains, it still gets its share, being, after all, the first land east of Japan.

Since sun, wind and rain are the factors that largely determine which plants grow and where, it would be expected that the Vancouver Island forests would vary markedly from place to place. But added to these elements are two more: the sea, which tends to warm the island up in the winter and cool it down in summer, and the mountains, which act like an icebox at all times of the year in addition to influencing patterns of sunshine, wind and rain.

Taking all these factors into account has proven to be a frustrating chore for those who map vegetation patterns. But the task though difficult is not impossible, and people who travel the island have come to recognize broad forest zones, each with characteristics setting it apart from its neighbour.

The largest zone lies to the west and is dominated by the western hemlock. No single tree can represent the island's forests, for they are too varied, but if one had to be chosen, this would be it. The hemlock is a pretty tree when young and magnificent in maturity. For the first few years of its life, it is slender and delicate, with a supple top that bends beneath its own weight. In old age the top still bends, but has long since grown out of sight except to birds and helicopter passengers. In maturity the hemlock can grow 300 feet tall and a dozen feet thick at the base, and contain enough wood to make several medium-sized houses —

Hemlock

except that hemlock is generally used for pulp rather than lumber.

The distribution of the hemlock can be explained by two factors — moisture and shade tolerance. The tree needs at least thirty-five inches of precipitation annually to survive and does very well with nine times that amount, making it ideally suited to the island's western region. But it peters out to the east where there is usually enough moisture only along creeks.

However, the presence of moisture is only one reason for the prominence of this species. Just as important is the fact that it can grow without direct sunlight, an absolute necessity if a tree is to survive beneath the shade of the forest canopy. A shaded hemlock does not grow well — it develops a shape something like a palm tree, and a 100 year old hemlock may have a trunk only a few inches thick — but the very fact of survival means that when an old one falls, a younger tree is ready to take its place. And that in turn means that no other species can take over its space in the forest.

When white men arrived the hemlocks were waiting, monsters massed on the slopes of the west coast ranges, growing without break from the edge of the ocean into the clouds. Most had been growing since at least the twelfth century when the last great island-wide fire occurred — an incredible conflagration which probably wiped out centuries of growth in a single once-in-a-millenium summer.

Since the oldest of the island's trees apparently began life about 600 A.D., it is reasonable to presume that the great twelfth-century fire had been preceded by another one about 600 years before. Is a pattern apparent, a pattern of fiery holocasts every 600 to 800 years? And if so, is it possible that the trees which greeted the white explorers were only the twentieth generation of hemlock since the ice age when glaciers a mile thick covered the land?

Some of these twentieth-generation forests are still present in the western portion of the island, and visitors can view them in their untouched state as the first white men saw them 300 years ago. There are now many scars in the forest, but there are also a few areas where a man can still stand alone on the shore of a lake and see the land as it once was everywhere . . . great forests cloaking the hillsides so thickly that nothing can be seen but huge trees soaring above the undergrowth.

The hemlock is only one of many species of trees found in the west coast forest. Near the coast there are giant Sitka spruce which often grow larger than the hemlock. Spruce seem built for the wind, for while a hemlock will quiver in the slightest breeze, the branches of the Sitka spruce stand rigid in the face of winds up to thirty miles per hour. Even their needles are stiff, with points as sharp as pins.

Alder crowding the edge of a west coast stream

Red cedar

The island's spruce forests became a focus of attention during the second world war when loggers sought them out eagerly for the manufacture of "Mosquito" fighter bombers — and as quickly deserted them when the war was over, for west coast logging can be tough at the best of times, and other species of trees are much more profitable.

Then there is the western red cedar, a species favoured by coastal Indians for the construction of buildings and dugout canoes. Trees can still be found with pieces chopped out of them by Indians testing to see if the wood was firm, and loggers sometimes stumble across half-carved canoes deep in the forest. They were abandoned perhaps a century ago when the white men brought irreversible change to Vancouver Island, and now they lie in the underbrush, moss-covered and forgotten but still recognizable. Western red cedar lasts a long time, but modern loggers are less enamored of the species than were the Indians, for cedar tends to die back at the top, forming a gnarled mass of dead leaders that renders the tree virtually useless for anything except pulp — and there are better trees for that purpose.

Also found in abundance are three species of fir trees commonly called "balsam" by residents even though true balsam fir does not occur on the island. They are mostly noted for their striking cones — heavy, tightly-packed, dripping with pitch and sitting upright on the branches like perching birds. Balsam tends to become more dominant at higher elevations and sometimes is the most common tree there.

The only other major coniferous species in the west coast forests are the yew (more common to the east) and two types of pine. The first of these, white pine, is usually noticed only because of the large cones which drop to the forest floor, since the trunk is not distinctive and the characteristic long needles are usually far out of sight overhead. White pine has a rather unusual distribution, tending to be scattered about singly in the midst of other conifers.

The second species of pine, shore or lodgepole pine, is more noticeable since it grows in patches and is smaller with branches that are closer to eye level. It is adapted to growing sites which are either very wet or very dry — bogs and rocky knolls — and flourishes where other trees find it difficult to gain a foothold. Close to the coast, wind and moisture combine to sculpt shore pines into "mushroom" shapes with thick, bushy tops supported on spindly and twisted trunks.

Alder

But the west coast forest does not consist entirely of conifers, for there is always alder. A deciduous species, alder occurs along all rivers and streams and besides being pretty with its whitish bark, is also useful to the forest ecosystem, fixing nitrogen in soils which have been leached out by heavy rains. However, the alder's main feature is its ability to invade areas recently opened by fires, slides or logging, often blanketing such areas with thick stands which block out other growth, at least temporarily, to the chagrin of loggers.

But while the trees are the west coast forest's most dominant feature, it is difficult not to be aware of the undergrowth. In fact, it cannot be avoided. The undergrowth is most in evidence at the start of any west coast walk when the hiker must make his first damp plunge into the forest. And the prospect is usually discouraging, for in most areas the trees appear to burst out of an appalling mass of tangled bushes impassable to anyone without a machete.

Two shrubs make themselves particularly apparent, depending upon location. The first is salal, a tough and stringy bush with shiny leaves often used in corsages. Surprising numbers of people derive a side income from salal, driving into the forests after logging hours and on weekends to pick a trunkful for sale to florists. But most people who

West coast forest vegetation
Top, left to right: devil's club, Indian hellebore, alder catkins; middle: salmonberry, elderberry, violet; bottom: trillium, blueberry flower, sundew

come in contact with salal do not think of corsages. They think of jungles.

Salal grows best at low elevations in moist locations, and in favourable conditions can reach well over the height of man. But since it needs some sunlight to survive, often only the upper portions of the plant are leafed while below is a tangled mass of intertwined branches, each pushing its twisted path towards the sunlight.

Those unfortunate enough to have to negotiate a good-sized patch of salal often find that the most efficient method of travel involves a sort of swimming action in which the feet never touch the ground. But the going is slow and hardly fun since the salal is usually either unpleasantly wet or tinder dry, in which case twigs, dead leaves and other debris can infiltrate even the most tightly-fitting clothing.

Salal has one redeeming feature: its pectin-laden berries, which are abundant in late summer and which make fine jelly. But few people sample them because of their rough texture and odd appearance. Or perhaps we have become so used to considering salal an enemy that we cannot conceive of finding some good in it.

Salal

If salal is not encountered upon entering the west coast forest, a thicket of salmonberry almost certainly will be, and it can be just as annoying to travel through. Salmonberry is closely related to the raspberry, and the two are quite similar except that salmonberry is much bigger and bushier, and its berries range in colour from light orange to deep purple. Like salal, the salmonberry bush bears edible fruit with berries that are pleasant tasting though bland. Probably because of their similarity to raspberries, salmonberries are more often picked than salal berries.

The west coast hiker may also encounter other berry bushes which can form thickets of some significance (another euphemism meaning that they stretch for miles). The best known of these are huckleberries, undoubtedly the favourites of most west coast berry connoisseurs. They come in two varieties, red and blue, with the red ones known as huckleberries and the blue ones known as blueberries. Both types are smooth, round and slightly tart, although their taste varies considerably from place to place and year to year. The size also varies, but on the average the berries are about the dimension of garden-variety currants. The bushes are usually about six feet high, although some will grow two to three times that size with a trunk nearly as thick as a man's wrist.

Another prominent shrub is the elderberry which also comes in shades

of red and blue. While most other west coast berries occur singly on the stem, elderberries grow in bunches and make an appealing display among the greens and browns of the forest. Both types of elderberry are

edible, although the red one is a bit unpalatable and affects some people adversely while the blue one is generally used only for making pies and jellies. But birds like them, and band-tailed pigeons in particular are inclined to gorge themselves on elderberries.

Also common in spots, especially at lower elevations, is the thimbleberry, a dense bush with a broad leaf resembling that of the maple. Its bright red berry, which looks like a flattened raspberry, is quite tasty.

But no account of the west coast forests would be complete without mention of devil's club, a shrub with a singular capacity to cause discomfort to the hiker. It will be encountered on almost any walk through the west coast forests, but does not stretch for mile upon mile as it sometimes does on the mainland and can usually be avoided.

Devil's club grows in thickets composed of individual plants that are often considerably higher than a man. Each plant consists of a gnarled, punky stem covered at random with spines and topped with large leaves similar to those of the thimbleberry. And each rib of the leaf also bears spines which can inflict festering scratches. For all this, it is a striking plant in late summer when a topknot of bright red berries appears, and it is extensively browsed by elk — thorns and all.

There can be too much bush beneath the west coast trees, but the people who do not give up at first sight are in for a surprise, for the problems tend to be only skin deep. All Vancouver Island's forests contain patches of thick vegetation which are difficult to negotiate and these can be troublesome, but you will discover that wherever the forest canopy blocks out direct sunlight, the undergrowth usually thins out considerably. Sometimes it completely disappears, leaving only an eerie but pleasant world of giant moss-covered tree trunks and fungus. Such spots are rare however — about as rare as the patches of jungle which can occur where light penetrates.

Away from the sunlight, the plant species also change, and the dense thickets of salal and salmonberry give way to blueberries, false azalea (a very pale imitation of the garden variety), and various ferns. All are attractive, and since they tend to grow in clumps with mossy ground in between, rarely give trouble to hikers. Such areas are not colourful — the few flowers tend to be small and wan — but the shades of green and brown are striking, and the walking can be thoroughly enjoyable because these spots are cool even in mid-summer.

The western forest contains other pleasures. A fallen log begins to rot and from it burst seedling hemlocks, only a few inches tall but thriving in the pure humus of the log. Or the same scene will be apparent a hundred years advanced in time, with the many seedlings having become two or three tall trees (for only a very few survive), their roots

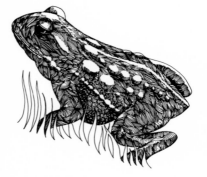

Toad

26

A red cedar growing in a young forest

snaking out and around the old log. Occasionally, the final scene will be apparent — a tall hemlock suspended on elevated roots from which the original log has rotted completely away. But such a sight is rare, for the forest floor generally builds up to surround the decomposing log and by the time it is gone, there is only earth to be seen around the roots of the tree.

Creeks, like trees, are endless in their variety. The larger creeks where sunlight reaches are choked with alder and salmonberry and salal. But in winter and early spring before the leaves are fully out, creek banks have a different look. This is when the spring flowers are in their glory, taking their brief chance to form seeds and survive. There may be yellow violets or white trilliums or perhaps a patch of delicate curly lilies, a species which grows in pink profusion along a number of west coast rivers and lakes. The curly lilies are known by many names — Easter lily, pink fawn lily, dog-toothed violet or Erythronium — and they are closely related to the yellow avalanche lilies which grow in alpine areas throughout the province. For most Vancouver Island nature-lovers, their blooms are the true sign of spring, and searching for them serves as an excuse to get into the woods for the first time since autumn.

For those who see a mature valley-bottom forest for the first time, the fungi are always surprising. Since fungi require rotting trees on which to fasten, and since most types take a long time to grow, they are usually absent where the forest has been disturbed. But in a mature forest, they can provide a welcome and unexpected show of colour amid the greens. Perhaps the most striking of all is the sulphur polypore which is bright orange and does not look particularly appealing, although in fact it is edible.

And there are other simple pleasures, such as breaking out of the forest onto a rock bluff, moss underfoot and a vista below, or the discovery of a great tree among the other giants, a tree that, placed in a forest of lesser trees might be world famous, but here is just one more tree in a seemingly endless forest.

The west coast, however, contains only part of the Vancouver Island forest, and although the hemlocks of the west are magnificent, it was the Douglas fir of the east coast that made the island famous among foresters.

Like the hemlock, the Douglas fir can be a true giant, 250 feet tall or more, but its bark is distinctive — a great corrugated chunk of wood perhaps a foot and a half thick with ten-inch furrows where the bark splits to allow the tree to expand. The fir's general form is very much like that of the Sitka spruce although the needles are not particularly sharp. But while both spruce and hemlock need a great deal of water,

Bright summer sun on a bracken fern

the Douglas fir can get by with amazingly little. Thus it is a tree that could not have been better fashioned for the eastern part of Vancouver Island which sometimes gets no rain at all in summer and where the creeks can dry up completely.

Unlike the hemlock, it needs sunlight to survive. But this has been no problem since fires have occurred perhaps every 100 to 300 years, and the flames have often simply weeded out old stands just as they were getting long in the tooth, providing fresh sunstruck country in which new fir forests could take root. In fact, the fires have probably been beneficial to the Douglas fir, for if they had not occurred, eventually a shade-tolerant species would have taken over. But the fires came regularly enough to be considered a natural part of the island's east coast ecosystem. Thus the fir forests existed when the first Indians arrived, and they still existed when the white men came milleniums later.

There are other differences in the eastern forests, perhaps the most striking being the more broken terrain. While many west coast valleys are dotted with cliffs and rock faces, such interruptions in the forest tend to be more prevalent to the east, resulting in a much more varied appearance.

This variety is most apparent in the trees, for on a single hillside there may be lodgepole pine, white pine, balsam, grand fir and yew as well as the ubiquitous Douglas fir. And in the valley bottom may be found alder, cottonwood, maple and western red cedar, the latter being less grotesque in appearance than those of the west coast forest because the climate is less severe here and the tops do not die back as readily.

However, the demarcation line between east and west coast forests is by no means sharp, for many west coast valleys have their complement of fir because of quirks of climate, and hemlock and spruce extend far to the east in many parts of the island, particularly in the north.

The undergrowth tends to parallel differences in the trees: under the Douglas firs it is generally less jungle-like and more park-like in the east, especially on drier sites. And while the shrubs tend to be similar, particularly in the wetter areas, there are a few species such as ocean spray, hairy manzanita and red rhododendron which are not often found towards the west. Ocean spray is a distinctive bush that can grow ten feet tall; it bears plumes of small white flowers in the spring but dries to a nondescript brown as the summer wears on. Hairy manzanita is a stubby, woody bush with reddish branches and grey-green leaves, often found with ocean spray, particularly at elevations above 1000 feet.

The rhododendron is perhaps the most spectacular of the east coast shrubs, however, for not only is it large (at times growing up to ten feet tall) but is as showy as the garden variety. On Vancouver Island

Moss grows thickly in the wet hemlock forests

East coast forest vegetation
Top, left to right: white Easter lilies, chocolate lily, satin flower; middle: prickly pear cactus, rhododendron, yellow monkeyflower and sea blush; bottom: kalmia, spreading stonecrop, arbutus

it is found in only a very few widely-separated locations, but in these locations it flourishes, an unusual distribution that has never been satisfactorily explained.

To the southeast the vegetation changes even more due to the drying trend which occurs as the Vancouver Island mountains flatten out into a narrow coastal plain which runs from Campbell River to Victoria. Driest of all are the Gulf Islands where grassy headlands appear in contrast to the dark forests which cloak the rest of the coast. Here, the Douglas firs are joined (and in some cases almost replaced) by two of the world's most distinctive trees: the arbutus and the Garry oak.

The latter is a true "Mediterranean" climate species, gnarled, massive and seemingly built to last forever. Its corrugated grey bark surrounds a rock-hard trunk that can grow to three feet or more in diameter with limbs that are equally massive, yet brittle and liable to snap before a strong wind. It can make do with surprisingly little water and will live for years on a rocky outcrop, growing hardly at all, but surviving nevertheless.

The arbutus is also tenacious but, since it can stand a slightly wetter climate, is a bit more widely dispersed. It prefers dry, rocky sites and, like the oak, grows tall and gnarled where it can and short and gnarled where it cannot. But its bark is smooth rather than rough, and orange rather than grey, and peels off in thin, parchment-like sheets. The shiny leaves last through the winter, making it one of Canada's few broad-leaved evergreens.

For a few weeks in the year, however, the oaks and arbutus are overshadowed by the dogwood, yet another east coast species which grows in dry locations. The dogwood is noteworthy for its flowers; in spring they provide the island's east coast with an almost deep south aspect, being fully as showy as magnolias. Dogwoods also bloom in autumn, although the flowers are more scattered and often marred by frost, but the real autumn show is provided by its leaves which turn blood red.

In the spring, the flowers of this coast are magnificent . . . chocolate lilies, sea blush, lady slippers, shooting stars, Easter lilies and dozens more. The shooting stars and Easter lilies are of particular interest because of the unique varieties which occur on the island. Whereas shooting stars elsewhere on the coast have slender, pointed leaves, most of the shooting stars of southeast Vancouver Island have more rounded leaves and the Easter lilies are actually the pink-fawn lilies of the west coast, except here they are white. (Both varieties are extremely limited in distribution, although they are usually common where they occur.) Also well known in dry areas but rarely seen elsewhere are camas, a blue flower with many blooms on a single stalk, and the satin flower, a

grass-like plant with delicate purple blossoms.

The east coast forest was totally unique but is now largely gone. Population trends have followed rainfall patterns on Vancouver Island with the driest areas attracting the initial settlers. So the southeast coast was occupied first, and where white men went, the country changed. They cut the oaks and ran sheep on the grassland, then moved into the coniferous forests. At first the trees were regarded as enemies, obstacles to farming, but they soon came to be recognized as potential wealth and now, a hundred years later, only scattered remains of the original east coast forest exist intact at low elevations. People have been everywhere, removing and altering. While the land is still beautiful, it will never again be the same.

A Garry oak, indicative of the east coast's Mediterranean climate

2/**Water, Fast and Still**

On Vancouver Island, water is never far away. No area lies more than twenty-five miles from the ocean, and rain is a constant factor everywhere except along the southeast coast. And even there, it is only the summers which are dry. The precipitation collects in ponds and puddles from mountain top to valley bottom, spilling down the hills in rivulets and creeks which widen into rivers and lakes at lower elevations, lacing every part of the island with an abundant supply of fresh water.

Rivers run in all directions out of the center of the island, snaking their way between the mountains to emerge into the sea wherever valleys occur. Largest of all is the Nimpkish system which drains the broad Nimpkish Valley in the north central part of the island, but each area has its major river, and each river bears its populations of salmon and trout. Every river system has a unique fish population — different species or runs occurring at different times. Even where waterfalls drop right onto the beach, preventing sea-run fish such as salmon and steelhead trout from moving upstream, resident trout are generally found above the falls, left behind after the last ice age or else planted by man.

But even if there were no fish in the water, the rivers of Vancouver Island would be of interest for other ecological and geographical features. Perhaps most noticeable is the colour of the water. Along the east

Silt-free gravel beds such as this have helped produce fine fish runs in the White River

36   *Spring salmon return without fail to the river of their birthplace to breed and die*

Coho salmon

coast the rivers are usually very clear, except after a storm when they tend to muddy up badly as they rise. The west coast rivers are even clearer, taking on a distinctive greenish cast because one can peer so deeply into them. The Taylor and Gordon rivers are well known for this feature, but it is common to other systems as well. Many of the smaller west coast rivers and creeks, however, originate in bogs and swamps and are the colour of tea, which renders them quite attractive, especially on a sunny day when they turn golden brown, often tipped with foam. But most people prefer not to drink the water unless there is absolutely no choice, for it looks unpalatable at best.

Green or brown or clear, the rivers are fed by hundreds of smaller tributaries tumbling out of the mountains, and wherever there are hills, there are waterfalls. The steepest and longest falls are generally narrow (and often dry in summer) since they occur high in the mountains before the creeks have had a chance to widen into rivers. But though they may be only a few feet wide, they form an impressive sight as they cascade down the slopes in sheets of thin white foam, half a dozen to a hillside in some spots, dropping hundreds of feet to the slower-moving waters below.

Occasionally a larger river will take such a plunge in its vigorous journey to the sea, and one good example is Della Falls. The volume of water varies with the season, but in spring Della Falls are a spectacular sight as the water tumbles 1440 feet into the Drinkwater River. The drop is broken by a ledge halfway down, but the setting more than makes up for this imperfection — steep slides and tall striated mountains and deep snow even in mid-summer. The falls were formed by a glacier gouging out the country just downstream from Drinkwater Lake, leaving the lake untouched in a high hanging valley where it is fed from all sides by glaciers and snowfields.

A unique waterfall is located just north of Nitinat Lake where the Tsusiat River empties over a sandstone cliff onto the beach below. Much has been written of Tsusiat Falls since they are one of the highlights of the hike along the West Coast Trail, and few people are disappointed when they see them close up. Like Della Falls, they are much reduced during dry periods, but even then form an impressive landmark visible from far out to sea as they dive sixty feet to the beach.

Similar smaller falls can be seen elsewhere along the coast. One of the most striking, which drains Crawfish Lake on Nootka Island, does not simply drop off a cliff but thunders down an incline to dump itself onto the beach.

Falls are common to every river on Vancouver Island, and in addition to being scenic they make a substantial difference to fish populations.

Some are obviously too high for fish to negotiate, leaving upstream waters devoid of sea-run species. Others are borderline, permitting fish to pass only under certain water conditions — and in some years these conditions do not occur because of drought, so that a whole run of salmon or trout may be left milling beneath the falls. Occasionally, falls will present a barrier to some species but not to others: steelhead trout can leap falls that baffle salmon, allowing them to make use of miles of upstream waters with no competition except from resident fish.

Lifetimes have been spent studying the ecology of streams, and the island's waterways are diverse enough to illustrate why. Probably their most interesting feature is the salmon run, for the spectacle of the old fish returning doggedly to a river to spawn and die has always been compelling. In few species are the inexorable cycles of life and death so strikingly apparent, but even here there are subtle differences in each species' freshwater requirements.

Chum salmon, for instance, spend only their first few months in the rivers, emerging from the spawning gravel in spring as newly hatched

Water reaches its lowest ebb in summer, and the streams become strikingly clear

Tea coloured water, typical of many streams originating in bogs

fry and then heading to sea almost immediately to feed and grow. For them, the most important feature of a stream is its amount of silt-free spawning gravel — silt-free so that the river's waters can flow freely through it, providing the buried eggs with enough oxygen.

All species require good spawning gravel, but coho and steelhead have additional needs. Since they remain in the river for up to three years, they must find areas in which to feed and suitable cover to allow them to escape predators. They also have rigid temperature requirements: if the stream gets too cold, they cannot grow satisfactorily; if it gets too warm, they die. Good steelhead streams have areas of large boulders to break up the currents, while coho thrive in wide pools and small back-channels where there are good feeding areas. And both need abundant streamside vegetation to regulate the water temperature and provide a source of food in the form of insects and other material which drop into the river.

Other species of salmon and trout ask still other things of a river. Sockeye salmon, for instance, normally spawn only in systems which contain a lake (presumably because it provides a suitable feeding area), while giant spring salmon usually lay their eggs only in the lower reaches of larger rivers. Springs gouge out three-foot deep redds to deposit their eggs, producing real hazards for anglers who may plunge into such holes unexpectedly while wading a river. Coho, in contrast, will run up a river practically onto the wet grass to spawn.

Lesser known species of fish which also move into the river from the sea include the lamprey, a primitive snake-like fish which clamps onto

A bog along the Tsitika River; a welcome opening in the mature forest

salmon or trout like a leech. The mouths of lampreys resemble suction cups, enabling them not only to attach themselves to their prey, but also providing an efficient, if unusual, method of travelling rivers. Being low on the evolutionary scale, lampreys cannot leap waterfalls with the force of a salmon, but instead edge up slowly, locking onto the rock with their mouths while gathering strength for the next short burst. They are ghastly looking creatures . . . but survival is seldom related to aesthetics.

While the life within a stream is fascinating, people are more often impressed by the form of the river itself, the patterns of erosion produced by thousands of years of swiftly moving water. There are rivers whose rock banks are rippled and crinkly like small waves, while in other places the waters have smoothed out the stone into flat slabs. Sometimes the river undercuts the bank, leaving huge overhanging chunks of rock; elsewhere a river will dig smooth holes in the stone along its banks — so-called potholes. Perhaps the best examples of these occur on the Sooke River where they are now part of a park and have become a cherished swimming area because the smooth rocks present a welcome change from the barnacle-encrusted beaches common to the island's coasts. There are also one-of-a-kind attractions such as the black banks of low-grade coal which lie exposed along the Chemainus River, or the hole into which the south fork of the Artlish River disappears only to emerge again a short distance downstream and continue its path to Kyoquot Sound.

Fossils are also common along the island rivers. And, as usual, man has added his own attractions: many streams boast Indian petroglyphs, although their locations are generally kept secret for fear of vandalism. They vary in quality and some are now barely discernible because of moss and erosion, but at their best they are powerful examples of native art — stylized graphics of men and animals carved centuries ago into living stone.

While Vancouver Island waterways are usually fast and violent, they are nevertheless often arrested to form lakes, some of them surprisingly large. The biggest of all is really a multiple lake, for the John Hart Dam at Campbell River merged Buttle, Upper Campbell and Lower Campbell Lakes into a single freshwater body almost fifty miles long. Many of the natural lakes are also large. Before it was flooded, Buttle Lake was approximately twenty miles in length, and Great Central Lake is five miles longer than that. Seven other lakes are all over ten miles long.

Nitinat Lake could be added to the list, but although it is called a lake on the maps, it would be more properly designated as one of the island's longer west coast inlets. It is open to the sea at the infamous Nitinat Narrows and thus is tidal, but the narrows are not wide enough to per-

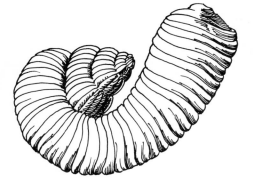

Fossil

Lamprey eel

mit total flushing of the fresh water, so the lake remains somewhat brackish. Because of its unique semi-salty waters it is quite sterile, too saline to support normal lake vegetation but too brackish to grow much in the way of marine life. It really comes alive only during the times when fish enter the lake prior to their final drive up the Nitinat and Caycuse Rivers.

Nitinat Lake stands alone among Vancouver Island lakes and inlets, but Henderson Lake (off the north side of the Alberni Canal) just fails to duplicate its effect. If the mouth of Henderson Lake were dropped by just a few feet, it too would be partially salty.

The island's larger lakes are ample testimony to the mountainous

Away from the light, the lower limbs of a Douglas fir wither and die

43

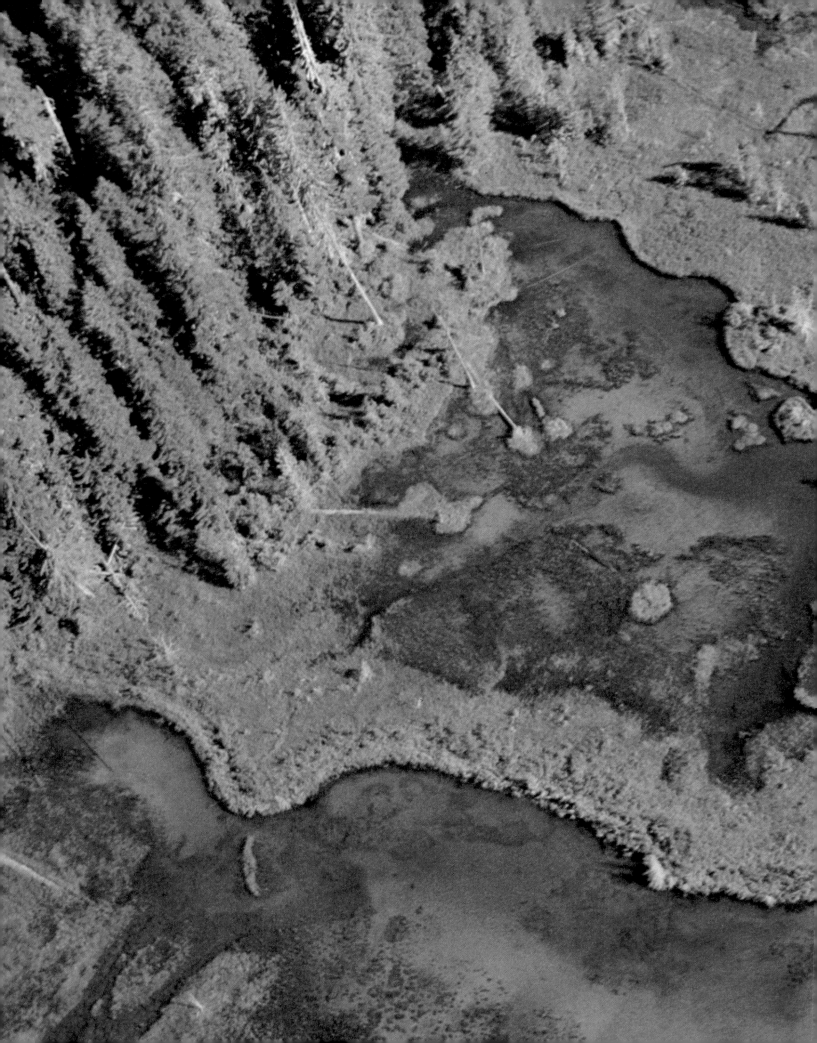

Petroglyph, Englishman River

nature of the terrain, for even on a map without contour lines, their shape indicates clearly that they are squeezed between long lines of hills. In fact the mountains generally rise so steeply that there is scant room for beaches and therefore the island's larger lakes have never gained the popularity of the ocean. They are too often rimmed by cliffs and when cliffs are absent, the forest usually crowds right down to the shore.

What the larger lakes have is grandeur — long sweeps of water with tall mountains stretching up from the shore — but many fishermen prefer the smaller, more intimate lakes where they need not fear the afternoon wind. And smaller lakes abound, hemmed in like the larger lakes by the forest, with shorelines rendered difficult for camping or other recreation by the presence of logs. These logs lie both in and out of the water, big old cedars which have been undermined and finally felled by the persistent wavelets, ending up dead and grey along the water's edge.

The undisturbed shores of the smaller lakes are usually lined with pondweeds and water-lilies where the water is shallow. Pondweeds are delicate floating things of many colours, lying limply on the surface and drifting with every wave. Lilies are more robust, poking themselves out of the water on stalks that are strong enough to support the weight of the plant if the water level drops beneath it. They form dense patches which can seriously impede a canoe, but they are easily avoided, and no canoeist would wish them gone in any case. Their stiff yellow blooms have a unique structure — yellow petals surrounding a pistil that is thick and pear-shaped — and they are colourful although rank smelling.

The prevalent water plants are indicative of a major difference between the smaller and larger lakes — acre for acre, the smaller ones are more productive of life. They are shallower, and pondweeds cover proportionately more of the surface, attracting waterfowl. A canoeist may often encounter a brood of ducklings poking about the reeds, or perhaps a nesting loon.

One area that could truly be termed "lake country" lies northwest of Campbell River, a region dotted with bodies of water which range in size from the Buttle-Campbell Lake complex down to mere puddles. Most are reasonably accessible over an extensive network of logging roads, and they have been well stocked with trout. Just as vacationers flock to Long Beach in summer, so the camper trucks pour into the Campbell River area for the fishing in late May, and few fishermen go home disappointed.

While the lakes are always popular, there are subtler waters for those with a penchant for natural history. These are the island's bogs, and they have a beauty of their own.

46

Previous page / Meandering streams in a bog along the shore of Stewart Lake

To most people the word "bog" has come to denote something dismal, a muddy swamp filled with unclean water, slimy creatures and nauseating stenches. Perhaps on the outskirts of cities, that is what bogs become. But in the forest a bog is a pleasant and fascinating place. It forms where there is an opening in the trees and may be a few yards or a mile in length, the result of poor drainage which prevents the normal forest vegetation from surviving. Instead, a completely different type of vegetation emerges, low shrubs and swamp grasses that can withstand the acidic conditions that would kill most plants.

For the hiker, the bog provides a chance to see the sun again after miles of walking under a coniferous canopy. It abounds with wildlife. Elk, deer, black bears, beaver, waterfowl and a host of smaller creatures all find conditions to their liking, and in some cases, essential to their survival, for bogs provide food. The pools and back channels here are rearing areas for coho fry, while the deeper waters often harbour larger fish.

A bog is a place totally unlike the forests which surround it, a place of surpassing beauty that is enduring despite its fragility. Woodsmen often call it a meadow, and while it is not a meadow in the strict sense of the word, somehow the name is more fitting than "bog."

Bogs are most common on the coastal plains, but they also occur in wide flat-bottomed valleys (often at relatively high elevations) and on mountain plateaus. They may be found near some lakes, but just as often there is no lake associated with the bog; it simply exists as an opening in the forest filled with meandering creeks and pools, flooded in spring but often dry in summer.

Because poor drainage is a relative thing, there are as many gradations of bogs as there are intermediate types of forest. At one extreme is the type which is under water most of the year, resulting in a region which contains little more than a variety of swamp grasses; while at the other is an area which is dry most of the time but is nevertheless wet enough on occasion to prevent the development of normal forest vegetation. This type of bog usually contains a number of distinctive shrubs such as cranberry and Labrador tea, a waist-high bush with thin shiny leaves, woolly on the underside and reputed to make a passable drink for those willing to try it.

Beneath the shrubs grow other bog species such as sphagnum moss, a pulpy species which is always soaking wet. Close examination reveals that each stem resembles a miniature palm tree, often with a reddish tinge. The sphagnum moss builds up in thick layers, gradually creeping out over open water until the surface becomes totally obscured. Those walking on a mat of sphagnum must therefore be cautious, for the water

is often just a foot or two below the surface and there is always the danger of plunging through this floating mat. Eventually, over thousands of years, the sphagnum will fill in a pond, self-destructing by eliminating the water. All that remains will be a small depression containing a grove of lodgepole pine, the coniferous species which can best tolerate the resulting highly acidic soil.

Pines are a characteristic feature of Vancouver Island bogs, and may be found right in their center on any sort of small knoll where the roots can get a purchase, but life is never easy in such circumstances and a two hundred year old tree may be only six feet tall. Even where the middle of the bog is devoid of trees, pines will generally be found around the perimeter, surrounded in turn by a ring of gnarled old cedars. Oregon crabapple, which makes a brilliant splash of red in autumn, and fleshy-leaved plants such as the skunk cabbage are also common. At the right time of year the distinctive kalmia is prominent, and further close examination of the vegetation will reveal the presence of such surprising smaller species as the insect-eating sundew, a tiny plant which exudes sticky dew-like droplets to trap its prey.

The most important thing about bogs is that conditions be "just right." An amazing variety of plants has evolved to handle the problems peculiar to existence in such areas, but each does best within a discreet range of moisture and acidity. Species tend to sort themselves out, forming concentric rings around the water: first the swamp grasses, then the shrubs and then the trees. In most bogs, however, one of the zones will be dominant because of accidents of geography. If the bog is dotted with small knolls, trees will be prevalent; if the bog is uniformly flat and poorly drained, only swamp grasses may grow. Sometimes, spaghnum moss will be the most common plant, or if the bog is drier, shrubs will have taken over.

Bogs of all types may be found almost everywhere on the island, but there are areas of concentration where they become dominant. The best known of these occur along the north and west coasts at places like Cape Scott, Tofino and Estevan Point, but the prettiest bogs are found in the high mountain valleys in the centre of the island — the White and Tsitika River valleys for example — simply because of the contrast they present to the tall mountains which surround them. Wherever they are found, they never cease to be a delight, even for those who know them well.

Tsusiat Falls, an impressive landmark along the West Coast Trail

Overleaf/Sphagnum moss, characteristic of bogs

3/ The Forest Animals

It is early summer and the overnight dew is still lying crystal-sharp on the blueberry bushes. Somewhere nearby a pileated woodpecker is hammering at the punky wood of a rotting snag, the sound muffled by the intervening trees. Down the valley a raven croaks and a brown creeper works its way busily up a tree trunk. And then, one by one and silent, the elk step out into the meadow.

This is what the Vancouver Island forest is all about, for while animal life may at times be sparse, the woods would seem empty without it. The hiker must often content himself with the knowledge that the wildlife is there even though he cannot see it, however, for the bushes and thick trunks permit an animal to escape easily from view. There will usually be only a quick hint of something moving in the bush, and then just the rustling of leaves.

This is true even of the birds, which are more frequently heard than seen. But although the animals are rarely on view, the island has a rich and varied fauna. And the animals have worked out patterns of living which seem to permit as many species as possible to share the same land peaceably.

The most significant of the island's animals is the Roosevelt elk, its largest terrestrial species. Only an expert would appreciate the small physical differences which distinguish it from its interior cousin, the Rocky Mountain variety. The real contrast lies in the life style of the beast — and that is a matter of circumstance rather than genetics, as indicated by the fact that Rocky Mountain elk transplanted to the Queen Charlotte Islands apparently behave in their new habitat completely like coastal Roosevelt elk.

Bald eagles congregate along the streams when the salmon are running

Roosevelt elk occur west of the coast mountains from California to Vancouver Island, making the island's elk the northernmost natural population. In historic times there were probably elk in most Vancouver Island valleys from tide line to the mountains, but hunting, logging and general interference by man have diminished their numbers until now they have vanished from many of their former haunts.

However, in some areas of untouched forest they still live as they always have, well in some years and poorly in others, but surviving. Life is never easy for animals at the geographic limit of their range and a constant struggle exists to provide their bellies with enough high quality food to enable them to survive. Conditions are best in the summer when the herds graze amid bogs and slides, putting on fat in preparation for the winter. Elk choose the vegetation in these areas because sunlight can get at it, significantly increasing its nutritive content, and they will stay as long as they can. In particularly mild years, at least some of the animals will remain in these areas all winter, but when heavy snows occur the herds are forced to retreat downstream to traditional winter ranges where they bide their time under tall trees, waiting for the chance to move back upstream.

Elk are often on the move, but no matter where their travels take them, they appear to prefer the valley bottoms. And where elk move, they inevitably grind out well defined trails along the rivers, always choosing the easiest route and incidentally making paths that men can use. In many areas the elk trails run over passes between valleys, forming routes that may be followed for miles, and which traditionally have been used by trappers and prospectors who help keep them open with axes and saws. Man and elk are often in harmony in the island's forests.

The habits of the Vancouver Island elk contrast to some degree with those of the interior variety. But it could be argued that the island's elk are typical in being different, for there are many differences between the fauna of the mainland and Vancouver Island, due, of course, to the water barrier. Not only has the water prevented a number of animals from reaching the island (among the more notable absentees are skunk, bobcat, fisher, long-tailed weasel, flying squirrel, porcupine, chipmunk, pika, snowshoe hare, oppossum, mountain goat and grizzly bear), but it has also allowed Vancouver Island mammals to evolve with enough distinctions from their mainland counterparts to warrant acknowledgment as separate varieties.

Two forest mammals are particularly noteworthy, both for their unique characteristics and the fact that they are considered by many people to be rare and endangered.

The best known of these is the Vancouver Island wolf which (like the Roosevelt elk) actually does not appear to be in any significant danger of extinction at present. There was cause for alarm some years ago when wolves suddenly declined dramatically in numbers, perhaps as a result of extermination programs. But by the late 1960s they were beginning to recover, and now people can hear them howling once again, and sometimes even sight them in the bush. Apparently the recovery is island-wide, for recent reports of sightings have been received from virtually all parts of the island.

There is less cause for optimism about the second rare species, the wolverine, although no real cause for alarm can be shown. The situation is simply that no one really knows much about Vancouver Island's wolverines. Perhaps their status is unchanged, that is, perhaps they were rare historically and they are still rare, but no one is certain since accurate records have never been maintained.

Wolverine

Like the wolf, the Vancouver Island wolverine is recognized as a separate subspecies on the basis of smaller size and darker colouration, but the differences from the mainland races are not significant enough to be noticeable to anyone but an expert.

Of other more abundant island mammals the deer are most commonly in evidence, officially known as coastal black-tails. They are classified as a subspecies of the interior mule deer even though they more closely resemble the interior white-tailed deer in habits and appearance. Like the white-tail they prefer the forest canopy to wide open spaces but, considering the island's vegetative patterns, they don't really have a choice.

They are much more widely distributed than elk (and that situation probably existed even prior to the time when man began to reduce the elk population), but where the two species co-exist, there are interesting behaviour differences which effectively ensure that they do not compete extensively. While the elk tend to be valley-bottom animals, the deer frequent the slopes, and there are probably subtle differences in diet as well. Both eat many of the same foods but each chooses different things as the mainstay of its diet.

However, it will be a long time before people understand all there is to know about deer and elk on Vancouver Island. For instance, no one has yet satisfactorily explained why deer appear more numerous in the east than in the west, and arguments seem destined to go on forever about the effect of man and his activities — primarily hunting and logging — upon the herds.

The only other large mammals native to the island are black bears and cougars, both of which appear to be doing well. Black bears have always thrived where they have access to salmon runs, and while they

Almost one-fifth of the world's trumpeter swans winter on Vancouver Island

are not exactly seen shoulder-to-shoulder along the streams in the autumn, they are certainly not uncommon. Cougars, meanwhile, should survive as long as the deer do. Cougars are never numerous, but the Vancouver Island puma population is probably the densest in North America.

Cougars occasionally prove troublesome on the island, killing dogs and cats, and on rare occasions even attacking humans. While there are no recorded deaths on Vancouver Island as a result of cougar attacks, there have been frightening incidents, some involving children. When such an attack does occur, it is small consolation to realize that most woodsmen consider themselves lucky if they obtain even a glimpse of a cougar in the underbrush.

The larger animals command attention, but by far the most common of the island's furry creatures is the shy but engaging white-footed mouse. This species, also known as the deer mouse, is rarely seen despite the fact that it is certainly abundant over most of the island. Because an animal as small as a deer mouse never manages to travel very far, its

A killdeer defending its nest

populations have evolved in many different ways, and those separated by geographic barriers show numerous distinctive characteristics. To date, close to a dozen subspecies have been described for Vancouver Island and adjacent islands; who knows how many more will be found in the future.

Other fur-bearing mammals abound: shrews and voles as well as the larger mink, marten, raccoon, beaver, otter and short-tailed weasel. In past years, they supported a widespread trapping industry, and loggers opening up the last valleys are still discovering abandoned trappers' cabins along the elk trails — mute evidence of a way of life that now has virtually disappeared. In addition to the native fur-bearers, foxes, musk-rats and cottontail rabbits have been introduced to the island, and all appear to have become established.

One of the most fascinating and smallest species is the navigator shrew. Because it looks like a ferocious mouse it is not a particularly attractive creature, although its black back and silvery-white underside is rather pretty. But the navigator shrew has its moments: such as when it walks on water.

It is stretching the truth somewhat to imply that this mouse-size shrew actually walks on the surface of the water but neither would it be accurate to say that it swims. Being so light, it rides the water like a piece of fluff, scarcely breaking the surface tension as it skitters about in the manner of a water spider. Nor does the navigator shrew confine its activities to the surface of the water, for despite the fact that animals of this type are usually strictly terrestrial, it has learned to hunt beneath the water like an otter or a seal. Because of size, however, it confines its prey to minnows and various types of water-dwelling insects.

While the water barrier has kept the number of mammal species to a minimum, the bird life more than makes up for any omissions. Vancouver Island has more avian species than any other area of similar size in Canada. Relatively few of these could be termed true "forest" species in that they will be found nowhere else, but conversely there are relatively few Vancouver Island birds that never venture into the forests.

The trumpeter swan, the largest of the island's birds, is a good example. Once close to extinction, the trumpeter has recovered under rigid protection and is now in the midst of a population boom. Nowhere is this more evident than on Vancouver Island where perhaps one-fifth of the world's total population of the species is found in winter — upwards of 1,000 birds. The bulk of the island's trumpeters apparently nest in coastal Alaska, moving south with the cold weather to spend the winter on suitable bodies of ice-free water on Vancouver

Island. Most of the birds end up on inlets at the mouths of rivers, but a substantial portion spends as much time as possible in lakes and ponds throughout the island. Only in the most extreme weather conditions are the birds forced to desert areas such as the Nimpkish Valley and Buttle Lake, and so it is realistic to include them among the birds of the forest. The same thing is true of other waterfowl species such as mallards, buffleheads and goldeneye ducks.

Many waterfowl also make use of forest lakes and rivers during the nesting season. There is substantial breeding by species such as Canada geese, mallards, pied-billed grebes, teal and wood ducks on the lakes and marshes, while species such as mergansers and harlequin ducks use the mountain streams. Wood ducks and buffleheads actually require forests for nesting since they breed in holes in trees. Great blue herons also nest in trees — incongruous for a big wading bird — while rarer ground nesting species such as the sandhill crane prefer the forest because of the seclusion it affords.

But the true forest birds are species such as grouse, thrushes, warblers, woodpeckers and various types of hawks and owls.

The blue grouse is a handsome bird and has always been closely associated with the island's forests. In spring the male perches in a prominent place, spreads his tail feathers, fills two air sacs alongside his neck, and assumes a glorious but grotesque pose. His ventriloquial "hoot" is produced to attract females to his territory and to warn other males that he means business. When not in use the air sacs become wrinkled orange skin and are normally covered by feathers.

At one time the island's blue grouse population boomed, and old hunters tell of being able to stand on one stump and shoot two dozen birds. Today, if a hunter sees half that many birds in a day of tramping, he will consider himself lucky. But it is doubtful that hunting had anything to do with the decline of the blue grouse, for the population appears to have been regulated by genetic means. While the theory is not completely proven, it is now thought that there are two types of grouse — some aggressive and some not. The aggressive birds demand larger territories than the non-aggressive ones, so that an area with aggressive grouse supports fewer birds than an area with docile grouse.

It is believed that at one time the island's massive populations consisted largely of non-aggressive birds. They colonized the burns and logging slashes of the 1930s and 1940s, but over the decades were gradually driven out by invading aggressive grouse, causing the present low populations.

The other member of this species found on the island is the ruffed, or willow, grouse, more a creature of dense forest than the blue grouse.

Great blue heron

Overleaf / Roosevelt elk near Paterson Lake; the northernmost natural population of this species is found on Vancouver Island

While the latter prefers openings in the trees such as those created by fire, the willow grouse chooses more bushy areas, usually along streams. Thus in virgin forests the blue grouse is confined largely to rock bluffs and alpine areas on the sidehills while the ruffed grouse is found in the valley bottoms. In many ways, the demarcation of ranges is similar to that employed by deer and elk.

Also in much evidence are the raptors — flesh-eating birds such as eagles, hawks and owls. The most common raptors are the bald eagles, found along the coast in large numbers at all times except when the salmon are in the streams, when they gather in amazing concentrations along the rivers to feast on the dying fish. The island also has a few golden eagles — true birds of the forest — and near the lakes and sea-shore, ospreys can be seen. Along the east coast an observant person will often be able to spot buzzards — turkey vultures — a species not often associated with the coastal forest, and which few people realize exists on the island.

Then there are the woodpeckers: sapsuckers, which drill holes in neat rows; giant pileated woodpeckers, birds as big as crows which tear great chunks out of rotting trees in their search for grubs, and tiny downy woodpeckers, scarcely bigger than a sparrow. And there are warblers, brilliant in colour but rarely seen because they hide among the branches; varied thrushes, shy birds like robins with black V's on their breasts; nuthatches, small insectivorous birds which walk head-first down tree trunks in search of food, and brown creepers, small nondescript birds which travel up the trunk of a tree instead of down it.

And the forest floor has its oddities: the grey jay, or Whiskey Jack, which almost never descends below 1,000 feet and which is so tame it will perch on a man's head to get a meal, and the water ouzel, often called the dipper because of its curious habit of bobbing up and down while perched on a rock in the middle of a rushing stream. It is a grey, short-tailed bird about the size of a robin and, like the navigator shrew, is a species which makes the most of the water despite the fact that it looks better adapted to dry land. To those unfamiliar with the habits of the ouzel, it is as startling to see a dipper suddenly dive off a rock into the water to search for insects as it would be to see a robin or a swallow suddenly disappear beneath the water's surface.

Just as some mammals have been introduced to the island by man, so have some birds. A few imported species like the starling and house sparrow spread to Vancouver Island after having been introduced elsewhere on the continent, but most of the imports were introduced specifically to the island. The most common of these are the Chinese ring-necked pheasant and the California quail, both of which have done well along

Pileated woodpecker

In summer, black-tailed deer may be found feeding in nearly any forest opening (Photograph by Barry Thornton)

the southeast coast and occasionally are reported elsewhere. They have become so much a part of the bird life, in fact, that most people forget they were not here originally.

There can be no better testimony to the uniqueness of the Victoria climate than the introduction of the skylark. It never expanded much beyond Victoria, the Saanich Peninsula and Duncan, but was doing quite well in these areas until subdivisions began gobbling up the fields in which it nested. If the building trend continues, the skylark will likely disappear — a significant loss, since it occurs nowhere else in North America.

Also of interest because of its rare status is the mountain quail, a species introduced near Victoria along with the California quail, but which never did as well. It is still hanging on here and there about the southeast tip of Vancouver Island, but many people are concerned for its

Overleaf/
One of the world's densest cougar populations is found on the island

future. The habitat is only marginally satisfactory, and it is quite conceivable that the populations will die out completely.

The island also has its garter snakes and alligator lizards (less fierce than the name implies) and a meagre collection of frogs, toads and newts. For the most part they are hidden from view, although during the breeding season toads seem to be everywhere along the river banks. And there are slugs, singularly repulsive-looking specimens three or four inches long when fully extended, interesting in their variety of browns, ranging from near white to near black. Some are spotted, while others will have a head of one shade and a body of another. Some shades seem to dominate in certain areas, and the most extreme colour combinations are more often seen on the west coast.

Finally, of course, there are insects: black flies and mosquitoes and tiny no-see-ums which make life miserable when conditions are right — or, more accurately, wrong. Most annoying of all are the wasps and hornets whose stings can prove fatal to those sensitive to their poison. But for most people insects are only an inconvenience, one more thing to be careful of in the forest, like devil's club. It says a great deal for the benign nature of the island's fauna that, in many ways, the insects are the most bothersome animals of all.

Mountain quail

Neat rows of holes in the trunk of a tree, the work of sapsucker woodpeckers

Alligator lizard

4/The Changing Forest

Fireweed covers the open spaces left by the burns

The forest is never a static place. Animals are born and animals die: trees fall and others spring up to replace them. And yet, for centuries at a time, there is an illusion of no change at all. Alders still hang over the rivers and sundews still catch tiny flies in the bogs; cedars still grow on the flats and elk still migrate in the winter snows. There are places on Vancouver Island where a walk in the forest is like a walk in time, for the explorers of the 1800s wrote of treks that seem identical to those that can be taken today and of experiences that a man could as easily have a week from now as have had two hundred years in the past.

Despite the minor patterns of change within the system — the death of a tree, the death of a deer — the forest endures. But sometimes the changes are cataclysmic. Lightning strikes, and for the next hundred years nothing will be the same. In the space of a few hours, the giant conifers will be reduced to smoking stumps and the green canopy will be harshly ripped away. Then the true energy of the forest is revealed, for almost immediately the rebuilding process begins and a pattern of change is set in motion which eventually, a century or more later, will leave the land looking as it did before the fire.

Annual plants will spring from the blackened earth in patches or as scattered, individual plants that can scarcely be seen from a distance amid the dark and bare rock. But they are there, and deer will be drawn to them in spring and summer.

Alders soon spring up after logging or a fire, crowding out other species

For a year or two or three, the annuals may be the only vegetation, although if the burn was not too hot, roots of some shrubs may have survived and shoots of salal and huckleberry may spring up. But even if the original perennials did not survive the fire, they soon start to seed into the area, and other perennials rarely found in the mature forest begin to appear. One example is fireweed, a spike of a plant that can grow ten feet tall and is familiar to all who have walked through Vancouver Island logging slashes. It is topped by a pink many-flowered bloom and at times will blanket whole hillsides in brilliant colour. Bee-keepers seek out such areas in which to place their hives, for this fireweed honey is praised far beyond the island.

Behind the forest of fireweed comes the forest of the berry-pickers as other shrubs gain strength and come to dominate the burn, gradually pushing aside the fireweed and the annuals. The huckleberries, salmonberries and thimbleberries return and expand their territory, tastier than ever because of the sun, and they are joined by other berries not found in the mature forest — black-cap, trailing blackberry and gooseberry. Black-cap is a curious shrub with whitish stalks and a dark berry that resembles thimbleberry but has a unique taste. Trailing blackberry is a vine-like species that bears fruit half the size of common blackberries, but even more delicious, while the best that can be said for wild gooseberries is that they are an acquired taste which few people acquire.

However, the berries too are doomed to a limited tenure, and after perhaps a decade and a half, the new forest begins to show signs of the long-term form it will assume. If natural reforestation has been successful, young conifers will be growing quickly, four feet in a year instead of the mere inches common to older trees, gradually pushing aside the other species that cannot climb up to get to the sun. By about the twenty-year mark, the new conifers will have formed dense stands that can be a real problem to walk through and which have choked out almost all other vegetation. But after another twenty years or so the trees start to shade themselves so thoroughly that the lower branches begin to die, and then it is just a matter of time until the mature forest reappears in its original form.

In the interim the burn is a different place, often in unexpected ways. The change from six-foot-thick cedars to saplings just ten feet tall is obvious, but not so obvious to those unfamiliar with a true mature forest is the absence of thickets of devil's club, or the rotting stumps lined with colourful fungi and cavities made by woodpeckers, or the beard lichen which hangs from mature conifers. Some of the vegetation comes back — the salmonberry may reappear although often in a different form — but some of it simply does not. It takes years to grow

Trailing blackberry

lichen and fungi and the young forest doesn't have that sort of time.

It is a natural cycle — the mature forest and then in a day the blackened earth and then in a century the mature forest again. But other natural cycles are also possible, and sometimes the system goes awry. If reforestation with conifers is not successful, the alders seed in first, blocking the conifers out. Or perhaps the culprit will be salmonberry or salal or thimbleberry. But whatever the species involved, the result is the same; the conifers become starved for light and grow slowly, sometimes not at all.

This change is not really a significant event in the life of the forest, but it has obvious significance for humans who don't live as long as trees. To the forest it is just a mere forty or eighty year pause in the cycle, a moment in which the alders are given time to have their way and die. For, inexorably, under the alders the hemlocks and spruce are taking root and reaching out and as the alders die, conifers are ready to replace them. Eventually the original forest returns like the tide.

Sometimes the cycle can be even more complex. It is obvious that the first tree to become established has an enormous advantage, since it will always have first access to the sunlight, and in the forest, sunlight is life. Thus it may be that Douglas fir, through happenstance or perhaps the design of man, becomes established on land that previously grew hemlock. Given such a start, a Douglas fir forest may emerge and dominate the landscape for centuries — but eventually insects or wind or something else will kill the firs, one by one. And, one by one, they will be replaced by hemlock, for only the hemlocks can wait, small and spindly but still alive, under a shaded forest canopy.

The cycle can become still more complicated if another cataclysm — fire or avalanche or windstorm — wipes out entire sections of the mature Douglas fir forest. Then the young hemlocks also may be destroyed, giving the firs an equal chance to reseed the area and eventually giving rise to yet another Douglas fir cycle. There are places on Vancouver Island where ecologists believe that this may have occurred time and time again, preventing almost on a permanent basis the return of the hemlock forest.

As the vegetation changes, so do the animals and birds. While there are some species that exist best in the mature forest (woodpeckers, for instance, since old forests contain proportionately more rotting trees), the majority do better where there is a mixture of habitats within usable distance. Deer in most parts of the island require mature timber both for food and shelter in winter and as a place to hide in all seasons, but, given a choice, they will feed in the open areas during the warmer months because of greater nutrition in the plants. Thus deer have tended to in-

Circular log booms on an island lake

crease in areas which have been burned, provided that they have had access either to some areas of tall timber in winter, or winters not severe enough to cause them significant hardship. Most animals, from insects to blue grouse to black bears, benefit from fires on Vancouver Island. And for some species, the benefits are total: insectivorous birds for instance, find that fires create vast feeding areas and they need not remain to search for food in winter when the denuded land sometimes resembles a stretch of arctic tundra.

Fire can therefore be considered a natural part of the forest ecosystem. But man has always imposed his will on natural cycles, and the forests of Vancouver Island have not been an exception.

When the first explorers discovered the giant conifers of Vancouver Island, they did what came naturally. They cut down some trees to fashion dugout canoes and totem poles and longhouses, and burned down others to increase the deer and grouse populations. But the Indians produced little significant change, since occasional fires have always occurred, and the odd tall cedar has always fallen. Even though the next explorers arrived perhaps 5,000 years later, they too found a forest that was essentially virgin territory.

The white men treated the trees in much the same manner as the Indians had, using a few and burning the ones that got in the way, except that when they set fires it was generally to expose the bare rock for purposes of mining exploration rather than to produce game. But the period when the white men regarded Vancouver Island's forests as a nuisance was soon over. They came to value wood too much to waste it in forest fires; instead, they destroyed fish streams to get at it. Now this period too is nearing its end. Loggers and the public as a whole are coming to regard the forest as something greater than the trees: an entity that begins with soil and sun and rain, and which includes many things of value in addition to wood fibre. People are beginning to realize that the forest has multiple values, and that some of these can hardly be described, let alone given a price tag.

However, the realization has come too late for most of the island's original trees, for while mature forests have always been a prelude to change, the changes of the past century have been catastrophic in relation to what went before. Not for perhaps eight hundred years have so many immense changes taken place within such a relatively short span of time, and the changes continue. Of course, mature trees remain, in some areas in great numbers. There are still miles of forest in isolated spots, particularly along parts of the west coast. But only one major east coast watershed, the Tsitika, remains unlogged from ocean to mountain top, and its value as a recreation area is much less than other east coast forests which have long since fallen to the saw.

For the majority of people, of course, the end of the mature Vancouver Island forest may not make much difference. They have never seen a mature forest or an entire river system untouched by human hands, and they likely will not mourn their passing.

Even the people who regularly walk the woods are not often aware of the extent of the changes that man has wrought in the island's forests. We see second-growth trees lush and green, sometimes a hundred feet high along the highways, and are impressed; but we are not seeing the forest that used to be. We see the odd patch of old monsters preserved on a few acres of land here and there, such as Cathedral Grove at the west end of Cameron Lake, and we regard them as freaks, aberrations — and so they are, but only in the present context, for the story of the island once included trees six feet thick and 200 feet tall and still growing. Trees perhaps 1100 years old and still growing.

The changes go deeper still. Even the old groves do not represent the forests as they used to be, for trees can be preserved on an acre or two of land, but a forest is more than that — it is space. A forest can be affected readily by events that happen far away. A single bulldozer churning the headwaters of a stream can damage an entire river by silting up the gravel where fish eggs pass the winter; or a forest can be decimated by an insect infestation that began two mountain ranges distant.

Deer

Hemlocks commonly get their start in the acidic remains of fallen trees

Many of the forest creatures need room to live and plenty of it. A herd of elk, for instance, may require twenty miles of valley if it is to make its traditional migration undisturbed, and for animals such as the wolf and the cougar the demands may be even more extreme. A single adult male cougar may need a 100 square miles of territory all to itself.

Thus a small stand of immense old trees cannot provide a true indication of what the forest was like, for it is only the trees themselves which are unchanged by the alterations in the surrounding land. As the animals change in the nearby areas — in numbers or in habits — they inevitably affect the undergrowth upon which they feed. Some plants are highly favoured as browse and are held back when animal populations are high, while less palatable species get a chance to break free. If the animals increase, the food plants will be adversely affected. When the animals de-

The removal of the mature forest leaves a tundra-like winter landscape

crease, the long-suppressed species may suddenly get a chance to grow, totally changing the look of the undergrowth. The game trails will grow back into west coast jungle, rendering whole areas impassable.

Even in areas which superficially appear unchanged, man has had his effect. However, the changes have been uneven, for the loggers naturally chose the most accessible regions first. In some cases, such as in the southeast portion of the island, logging of the old-growth forests is almost finished, while in a few other areas it has not yet begun. Logging methods have altered greatly over the years and the evidence is clearly visible to those travelling the island's backroads. There are great star-shaped scars covering half a hillside, often filled with alder, caused by dragging logs towards the central spar tree on long cables. Or there are chutes where logs have been skidded down mountainsides into the water,

The remains of an old forest after a fire, with new trees already growing

and there are logging roads, phenomena in themselves for those who have driven only on pavement. In places they cling like eyebrows to the slopes, steep and forbidding, and people shake their heads at the courage of truck operators who will wheel sixteen-foot wide rigs around hair-pin bends, even in the snow, knowing that every so often the brakes fail.

Sometimes the roads occur in closely-packed clumps, whole hillsides or valleys covered with writhing spaghetti-like scars, or else they will be so tight together that they look like the prongs of a fork. These are the result of setting-access logging, in which the wood is retrieved by bulldozer rather than high-lead cables.

The changes in logging practices are also visible on a larger scale. Evidence may still be seen of the patch-logging of the early days when the loggers alternated clear-cuts with patches of timber. But beginning in the 1950s, patch-logging was replaced by progressive clear-cutting, in which the effect is similar to that of a scythe working outward in ever-widening circles, mowing all down before it. The result was the complete denudation of valleys and hillsides in some of the more heavily harvested areas. In other areas a crown of timber was left on the ridges, but all the lower elevation wood was taken.

Until recently, progressive clear-cutting was the most common type of logging on the island, and deer and elk populations suffered, for the removal of the lower elevation trees left no places where the animals could escape the winter weather. The deer herds are thought to have declined dramatically over much of the island as a result of these practices, and there is little prospect of their returning to former levels in the near future. However, logging plans now call for patch logging, and wildlife populations should be protected from harm in the future.

Even in areas that have been completely denuded of tall timber, the future can only bring better things for the wildlife because in time, the mature forest always returns. It might take a hundred years or more, but it is sure to come.

Overleaf/
Cedar stumps and new alder in elk winter range along the Elk River

5/ The Year of the Forest

The trouble with the Vancouver Island forest is that just when a man thinks he is getting hold of it, it changes into something else. For the forest is a place of rhythms, of cycles, a place where small changes overlay larger changes which overlay changes even larger yet.

The most important rhythms are geological, the massive forces which change the forest by moving mountains and shifting coastlines, changes which over centuries have produced the hemlock forests of the west and the fir forests of the east, and which in the future will change the forests yet again. But these changes are noticeable only in retrospect, a story written in rock that most people do not take the time to read.

Much more important to men are the cataclysmic changes induced by fire or logging, although even they may not be noticed by those unfamiliar with the forest unless they actually see the trees fall.

More obvious are the daily rhythms, the wind of the afternoon and the dew of the morning, the constantly-changing patterns of storm and sunshine which make the forest a place of endless variety, but which rarely have consequences lasting beyond a particular day because they are constant facts of forest life. A summer rainstorm may affect the forest for weeks to come, filling the creeks and bogs and preventing drought — but such storms occur every summer and the only matter of real consequence to most people is whether such storms occur during the one day when they are in the bush.

A tree falls in today's wind, but trees always fall. A deer browses peacefully in tomorrow's sunshine, but the sun always shines. An earthworm moves an inch of the forest soil, but time moves it back, and even though the day's events may seem important at the time, they have little consequence in the long-term life of the forest.

Such events as a summer storm really form part of a different set of rhythms, the rhythms of the seasons, which to those living in the forest are the most noticeable rhythms of all.

Most people see the forest in summer, and they find that even in that

Spruce trees reach an immense size in the western forest

Winter on the Big Qualicum River

peaceful season it has its moods. Shafts of sunlight will poke through the canopy of trees, turning the leaves of salmonberry translucent and silhouetting the salal. A morning mist will rise lazily from a lake as a pair of wood ducks poke among the bullrushes, while the mountains loom stark and magnificent, tight behind the water. Or a light summer drizzle will drift down out of grey skies that hide the peaks in banks of stratus clouds, reducing the forest view for a few days to the immediate trees.

Moods . . . but the moods do not matter, for the summer forest never changes much. By late August the valley bottoms are choked with vegetation in the new forest as well as the old, and the coho and steelhead trout are in the midst of their annual struggle to survive low water in the streams.

In the marshes and along the river edges, the skunk cabbage will be three feet tall, where it has not been nipped off by elk or bears, great fleshy leaves that seem more suited to the tropics than to Canada, its large spring blooms only a memory. The salmonberry will be higher than a man's head, a green filter for the sunlight that sifts through the trees, and a hiker will stop for a moment of pleasant observation and forget the thorns that await him in the thicket.

On the hillsides too, a summer walk in the woods is an enjoyable thing. The forest floor will be dense with salal in spots, but in other areas it will be covered with red and purple huckleberries. Like the bears, a person can browse for miles, taking in the sights and the berries at the same time. The only difference is that for the bear, feeding is a matter of necessity; forest survival is a sometime thing, and the animals must make full use of summer if they are to survive the coming winter.

But while there are dense thickets on every hillside and valley, in most places the forest is clear, with only deadfalls to impede progress.

Of course, summer is also the fire season and the woods become crackling dry in many places, particularly along the southeast coast. Sometimes the forests are closed and even when they are not, a camper must still be careful with his matches. Dry twigs and leaves work their way into boots and other clothing, the sweat trickles down and mosquitoes are always present. But it is cooler under the trees than in the direct sunlight, and the taste of a mountain stream is something to be savoured. There are a thousand gullies to be investigated, out-croppings to be climbed, views to be enjoyed.

Even in the logging slashes, August is magnificent. Greenery and flowers are rampant, a hundred species of plants for every dozen that exist under the canopy. Fireweed will stretch for miles in the big clear-cuts, tall and pink and often thick with honeybees. White puffs of pearly everlasting will dot the roadside, and all across the hill the berries will be ripe and ready for picking. Now, too, the fresh tops of the young conifers will be slowly straightening themselves after a season of furious growth.

It is a time of plenty, with fawns tagging at the heels of the doe, and nighthawks swooping as they gather in migratory flocks, and bats fluttering in the evening. Careful use of binoculars in some areas will reveal forty or more deer in a logging slash, heads down and browsing steadily at the edge of the trees; just after dark there may be seventy-five more. The forest creatures are fat, and growing fatter still.

Late summer is the time to get to know the Vancouver Island forest, but summer is soon over and the nights quickly become cool. One morning in September there will be a dusting of frost in the dawn, and the forest is changing once again. A few of the less hardy plants begin to die; leaves begin to loosen on the deciduous trees.

By mid-October the process is well underway. Now the forest has its moment of gold before the coming winter. The coast forest does not boast many reds in autumn — Oregon crabapple in the bogs, dogwood and blueberries on the hillsides, a few species of water plants — but the yellows and golden-browns of the maples, willows and cottonwoods seem accentuated by the sombre green conifers, and on the slides they can make quite a show.

As the trees change, so do the animals. The interior valleys echo to the weird bugling of challenging bull elk in September, but by the end of October the bulls are silent again, and may already be starting to desert their harems in favour of a solitary winter existence. The deer, so visible in August, have become shy and secretive even in areas where there are no hunters to frighten them. Where a person could count a hundred animals in the summer, he will be lucky to find two or three by mid-October.

The birds, meanwhile, have separated themselves into those that will migrate and those that will stay.

Because the lakes are always frozen and the new snow always falls, making food scarce, birds throughout most of North America have developed traditional migratory patterns that never seem to change. The geese rise from the shores of Hudson Bay and head south, perhaps to Louisiana, while the whooping cranes desert Wood Buffalo Park for Texas. The bobolinks and swallows and hawks similarly head south in great waves, leaving the north a barren place in winter.

But in British Columbia the migration pattern is as often to the west as to the south. A great many species such as warblers and humming-birds head south on a regular basis as they do throughout the rest of Canada, deserting Vancouver Island in late summer or early in September,

Autumn colour along the Megin River

but just as many begin arriving at that time from Alaska and the interior of the province, for the island is a major wintering area for a great many of the hardier birds.

The habits of many of these species are much less fixed, however, and they will move in response to local weather, shifting south in the face of a storm, then drifting back northwards again. Since Vancouver Island lies right in the middle of the area where such shifting commonly occurs, it is difficult to notice the patterns. Pintail ducks may move south to the United States in response to a January storm, but at the same time other pintails may move in from the Queen Charlotte Islands.

The migration picture is further complicated by the wide variety of habitats found on the island. Waterfowl using the interior lakes, for instance, can easily shift themselves into more hospitable conditions merely by moving a few miles down to the coast, returning as soon as conditions permit.

The island's bird life changes markedly with the seasons, and late fall becomes one of the best times for observation because that is when many of the major changes occur.

The trumpeter swans begin moving in from Alaska, small flocks appearing suddenly on suitable lakes and marshes all over the island; with them will come the ducks — bouncy buffleheads, bluebills, and goldeneyes, stark black and white and riding on whistling wings. Chickadees and kinglets will suddenly seem more prevalent, but other birds will seem less so even if they do not leave the island. The blue grouse, for instance, is a year round resident, but it disappears from the logging areas in autumn and heads into the mountains because unlike most species of birds it prefers a colder area in winter. It is truly a contrary species, for it ridiculously prefers to walk rather than fly to its winter habitat. People hiking the forests in autumn sometimes run into migratory flocks walking determinedly uphill and wonder what it is all about — but who could explain a behaviour pattern as curious as that?

In the rivers, meanwhile, the annual salmon migration approaches its peak in mid-October. Each species of salmon and trout makes it run at the rivers at a different time of the year, but by October and November the rivers may contain four or five species of salmon — some up to seventy or eighty pounds — and three or four types of trout.

Even without the spectacle along the rivers, many people find this the best time to visit the forest. The mushrooms are up — although they may have been nipped off by deer — the insects are gone and the falling leaves reveal unsuspected objects and vistas. A thrush's nest will be found in the branches, or a cave revealed behind a patch of salmonberry bushes, or perhaps the sea will suddenly become visible through the trees.

Bufflehead duck

But then it is November, and November is the month of storms. On the coast the wind will blow into the seventies at least once during the month, and islanders come to expect lashing rain and trees crashing down and creeks turning into brown torrents. At higher elevations the November storms bring snow, hurrying the deer and the elk on their way to wintering areas.

November can bring snow to the entire island, but such years are rare . . . indeed, in many winters the coastal fringes never receive snow at all. Higher on the slopes, however, snow is as certain as November storms on the coast and by mid-December only the coastal plains will still be green.

By December most of the Vancouver Island forest is a very different sort of place, a place that will become increasingly alien for at least six weeks before the weather begins to turn again towards spring.

At its lower edges the snowpack is variable, melting back one day and moving far down the hillside again with the next snowfall — light and fluffy on the day of the storm, soggy the next, then frozen solid by a snap cold spell only to be made soggy again by a sudden rise in temperature. In the interior valleys the snowpack is a permanent winter fixture, building to perhaps eight feet deep over the course of a severe winter, covering the salal and salmonberry and huckleberry without a trace. The logging slashes that were lush and green in summer resemble a barren Arctic wasteland in winter — great white expanses of snow through which poke only the tops of young conifers, or perhaps no growth at all, and which are totally deserted by wildlife because there is nothing to eat and the snow can provide a fatal trap.

This change occurs gradually, for the snowpack takes time to build up. Snow sifts into the forest gently through December, an inch or two today, six inches tomorrow, and sometimes a foot and a half during a particularly severe storm, large soft flakes which are usually just a few degrees away from being rain, packing even as they fall. But sometimes the snow comes with fury, small hard crystals riding an icy northern wind, and this snow does not pack. It will remain as powder for as long as the cold spell lasts, draining energy unmercifully from any animal forced to move in it. And they all must move: the search for food never stops. An abnormal year will come every so often when the temperatures hover below twenty degrees Fahrenheit for weeks. It is then that the animals struggle hardest, and many do not survive.

In conditions such as these, food becomes a matter of life and death for the deer and elk rather than something to pick and choose. With few bushes above the snow, they eat what they can, and sometimes it is precious little.

Sulphur top mushrooms

An early morning mist along the Gold River

Now the trees that blocked off the summer sunlight come to their rescue, for branches snap off in the inevitable winds, or whole trees fall, or lichens and mosses are torn loose from the limbs to drift onto the snow. The animals fall upon them eagerly, stripping the lichens and mosses and even the needles off the fallen branches in a desperate attempt to fill their stomachs.

But the fare is meagre at best and the deer and elk lose weight steadily, burning fat stored during the mild months of summer. The severity of the winter therefore becomes critical; the animals can survive such a downhill trend for only a limited time before the die-off begins. When this happens the animals struggle and flounder in the powder, eventually giving up and crawling under a tall conifer to die. Being weaker and less able to compete successfully for food, the young go first, and then the very old, preserving the nucleus of the herd. But even the mature adults will die in distressing numbers during a severe winter.

In spite of this continuing struggle, the winter forest contains much beauty. The bogs, so green in summer, become humped with thick white mounds as the snow builds up on the dry parts and melts away in the wet places, at least until the water freezes. The snowdrifts under the trees form smooth white contours against the thick trunks, sculptures of snow which are finally locked in place by the cold, frozen so solidly that on many days a man can walk without leaving a footprint.

This freezing of the snow is characteristic of Vancouver Island, a product of erratic changes in temperature brought on by the conflicting forces of mainland and ocean weather. While cold temperatures generally prevail in the island's interior in mid-winter, every so often the freezing level will shoot up to mountain-top height, 5,000 feet or more, turning the snowpack into a soggy mess. This process is aided by the fact that such rising temperatures are usually accompanied by fierce rains.

But thaws are only temporary, for the freezing level inevitably descends again, turning the soggy snow into something almost as hard as ice upon which the deer can walk, giving them a chance to reach new food. Yet the ice is never permanent, for the freezing level will just as inevitably go up again a day or a week or a fortnight later. The snowpack is constantly changing from day to day and year to year as a result of a host of interacting factors too complex to be adequately charted.

As early February approaches, the periods of melt usually begin to exceed the periods of snow build-up or freeze, and the snowpack declines. At lower elevations the snow starts to recede back up the hillsides, while in the mountain valleys a period of day-time melt and night-time freeze commences that generally reduces the snow along the edge of the waterways. This allows elk to move up the valleys, using the rivers as highways.

Through ensuing weeks winter's grip gradually loosens, and often by the end of March the logging slashes and bogs will be bare at lower elevations, permitting small herds of deer to congregate for their first nutritious food in months. And on the coast the early blooms appear, heralding the approach of spring.

Spring is slower in coming to the interior of the island, for while the waterways gradually open up, the forests remain locked in a thick blanket of snow. The first signs of spring are found near the bogs, initially with the disappearance of the snow in the wet areas, and then with the appearance of the yellow blooms of the skunk cabbage which poke their way through water and accumulated winter litter as soon as the snow is gone. The elk and deer and bears search them out, nipping avidly these first green plants.

Soon the forest is well into spring and the creeks begin to warm, permitting salmon fry to escape from the gravel and start a summer of voracious feeding even as the first of the steelhead begin their summer run into the rivers. It is a delicate time, a time of pastel colours. Sap starts to flow and buds begin to swell and burst. Branches assume subtle shades of yellow and red and purple, and in the emerging greenery each separate shrub can be distinguished because each wears a separate tone of green.

But the coming of the leaves spells the end of the ground flowers, which can find sunlight only in the short time between the melting of the snow and the rising of the sap in the trees. Their time finished, they drop their petals as the seed-pods swell. Before their seeds fall, they will be completely hidden by the new leaves of summer.

As the flowers disappear, the animals emerge. In addition to deer moving into the logging slashes, frogs begin to croak, toads are everywhere for a day or a week and masses of salamander eggs suddenly appear in the ponds. It is the nesting season, and the winter silence is broken by the sound of birds announcing their territories: robins chirping, flickers hammering on snags, ruffed grouse drumming with a sound curiously like a car starting and blue grouse hooting from stumps and rock bluffs.

In the hills the last bears shake winter from their coats and emerge from their dens with their cubs, while on the coast black brants will have moved in by the tens of thousands to loiter along the beaches till mid-May, when they will lift off northward again. The people who took their children to watch the salmon spawning in November now take them to the beaches to see the brant and listen to their gabble as they search for eelgrass when the tide is right.

Black brant

Skunk cabbage, one of the earliest flowers of spring

Suddenly it is early June, the birds are on their nests, and the deer and elk have slipped away — the females to bear young, the males to return to their separate summer ranges. Now, once again, the weather becomes critical. An unseasonably wet June can kill young birds by the hundreds as their parents huddle over them, unable to search out insects, letting them starve while attempting to keep them warm. And fawns may develop pneumonia in the chilling rain, to die a cold death in the swimming season.

Although there are always some young animals which will die, most survive, and the process continues. People are seldom aware of this animal mortality unless they chance upon the pathetic remains, for death in the forest is rarely a visible thing.

But while death is never absent, it is at a low ebb in summer. The cycle of the year has ended, even as a new cycle begins.

Previous page/
The winter snow completely blankets the underbrush in the interior valleys

The twisted roots of a windfall tree with a young maple already gaining a foothold in the forest clearing

Overleaf/
Rugged Mountain, less than ten miles from Tahsis Inlet on the west coast

II

THE MOUNTAINS

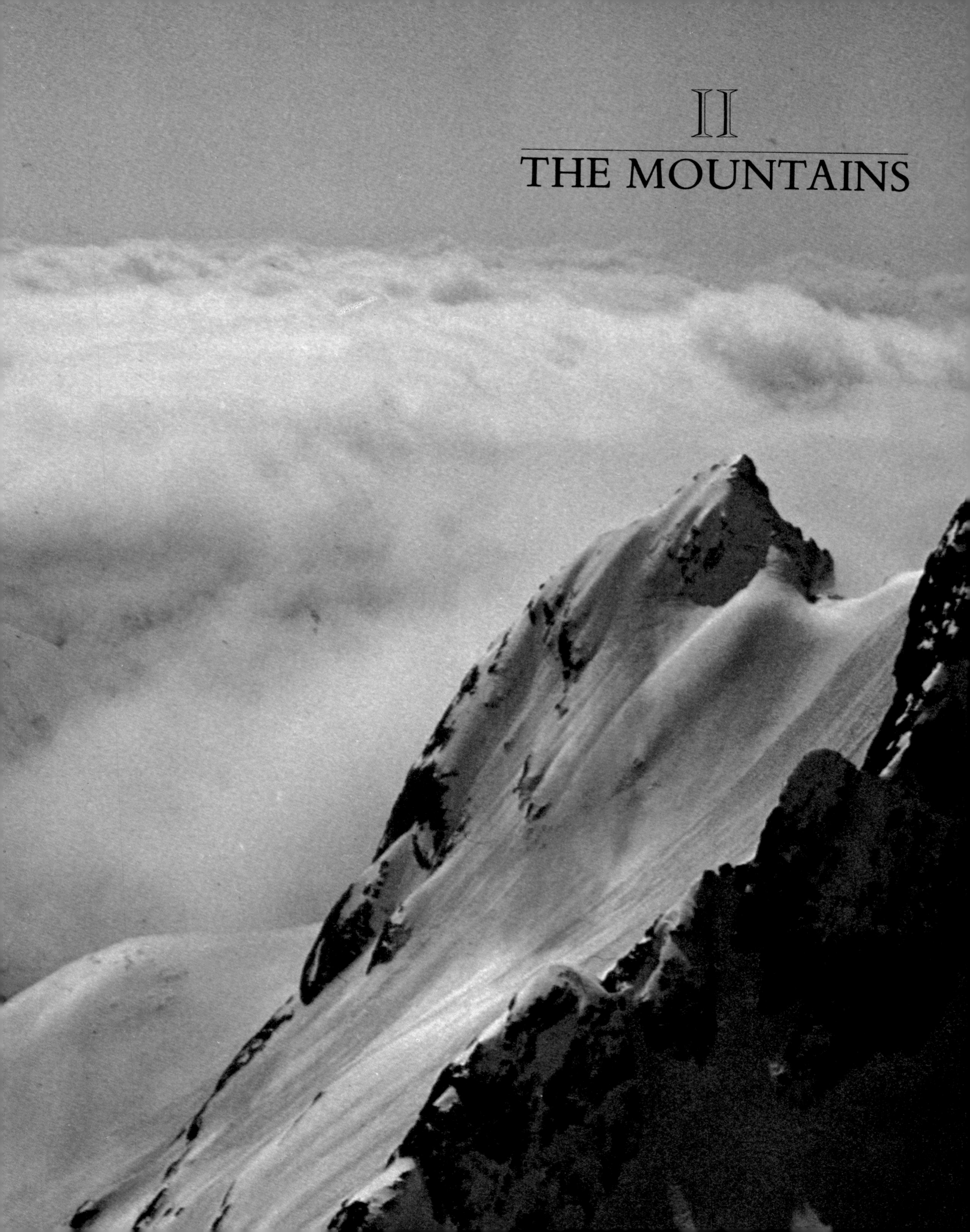

6/ The Top of the Island

*Ridges often run for miles
in the island's "little mountains"*

Beyond the forests and most of the roads lie the alpine regions of Vancouver Island, the most fragile of the island's environments but so far the least changed.

The forests are huge and they held enormous wealth, yet it took men less than a century to change them forever. The ocean, too, originally seemed too big to affect significantly, but the changes have come; years of fishing and stream destruction and seaside development have taken their toll and now the spectre of polluted waterways looms ever more serious, including the threat of inevitable oil spills.

But the alpine areas have been the site of only limited commercial ventures — a few mines, the odd ski resort — and access is difficult, so perhaps the flower-strewn slopes and delicate lakes and massive crags will avoid the pressures which have developed below. Of course, the threat is there; miners have already staked their claims over the mountains, including those of Strathcona Park, but so far mines are rare, and most of the options may never be exercised.

Difficult access has made the alpine areas the least-known of the three major types of habitat on Vancouver Island. Yet the mountains are really the dominant feature of the island landscape. The peaks lie in jumbled confusion over the land, defying pattern, with minor ranges running in all directions, and giant crags rising inexplicably from relatively level ground. If there is any pattern at all, it is obscure and difficult to discern. But it is present.

The cartographers began by naming a few peaks and ranges, then gave up and lumped them all under the label of "Vancouver Island Mountains,"and not without reason for, with the exception of a few scattered lowland areas and plateaus of varying description, the island really is composed of one big mountain range. It is difficult to compre-

Avalanche scars are common in the steeper areas

hend the extent of the mountains, the massive area that they cover, and their sheer magnificence on a clear day.

The island's peaks have been called the "little mountains" for they could be considered miniaturized versions of much larger alpine areas elsewhere in the world; often a 7,000-foot Vancouver Island peak will possess all the features of a mountain twice its height, except that everything is on a smaller scale. They dwarf the hills of the British Isles and are comparable in elevation to the Urals of Russia and most of the ranges of Italy, Greece and the Scandinavian countries, but they fall far short of even the coast mountains just across the water on mainland British Columbia, and are miniscule in comparison with the world's higher peaks. Nevertheless, names like Victoria Peak, Mount Golden Hinde, Mount Schoen, Mount Arrowsmith and Rugged Mountain have significance for those who have seen them, and they are impressive in their own right.

Perhaps it is the element of surprise which endears the mountains to island outdoorsmen — to emerge into green and flowered alpine meadows after hours of trudging beneath tall trees is like pulling back a curtain on the world. Sudden and unexpected vistas are revealed, both above and below. Perhaps it is the contrast, the stark and jagged peaks standing out above the gentle lowland contours of the island — bare rock and ice above thick forest. Or perhaps it is merely the overpowering number of mountains, the fact that while from below the peaks appear isolated and unimportant in comparison with the mass of the forest, from above it is the forest that is dwarfed. It is possible to look for miles and see only snowfields and rock, and it becomes apparent that the island's magnificent forests are contained only in slivers of valley which take up very little room at all. Here, the island is found to be a place where snow in July is the rule rather than the exception, a place of near-permanent ice where lakes may not be open until August — and in some years, not at all.

It is a place where one can walk for miles on ridge-tops and find no trees over twenty feet tall; a place where the devil's club and salal of the forest can be forgotten in the pleasure of walking in alpine meadows filled with stolid heather and ephemeral mountain flowers; a place where trout rise in shallow lakes to snap at anything thrown their way, for they have seldom been fished and must feed when they can.

The most impressive sights are the torn rocks and the snow and the alien vegetation — perhaps the vegetation most of all, for it is completely unlike anything found in the forests below. Gnarled by poor soil and cold and smashed flat by wind and sun, it forms a ragged blanket which more than anything else indicates the fury of the mountain climate. Yet it is spectacularly scenic. And above all, it endures.

Copper bush

The beginning of alpine habitat usually occurs at somewhere near 4,000 feet in elevation where the first hint of the transition comes with a thickening of the underbrush. After climbing through a zone of upper-elevation forest (often balsam) which sometimes contains no underbrush at all, the hiker suddenly finds himself encountering a totally new shrub, copper bush. It has flaky bark and yellowish leaves and grows in tangled thickets which often bear evidence of having been matted down under heavy snow.

About this time, too, the lowland trees will have been replaced by higher-elevation varieties. Balsam fir may still be present, but it will be stunted, while yellow cedar and mountain hemlock replace the western red cedar and the western hemlock prevalent below. Both resemble their lowland counterparts, but are bushier and usually much smaller. Larger species such as Douglas fir will have long since been left behind.

A few more yards of elevation, and the hiker will begin to spot the occasional patch of red heather, and soon, often mixed with white heather, it will form a carpet. At this point the forest canopy disappears completely in favour of small bush and isolated single trees which become more and more scattered until they no longer grow because there is only rock. On some sunny areas there will be patches of crawling juniper, a tree which grows flat like heather. But it is not really a true alpine species, for while it is found most commonly above timberline, it is also found as low as the 1,000 foot level on some dry hills.

As the trees diminish, the flowers increase, growing in every available pocket of soil where there is even a hint of moisture. In some slide areas there is no real shortage of either, and the entire hillside becomes a mass of flowers, although they are not always visible from a distance.

Up close, however, the flowers cannot be denied and visitors can spend hours examining the varied blooms in detail. There will be lupin, bush-like with spikes of blue blossoms which gradually turn purple as they begin to wither; or patches of purple penstemon, a bell-like flower which lies tight to the ground in brilliant mats, the blooms completely hiding its leaves. There will be composites of a dozen colours — purples and yellows and oranges and whites — and occasionally fields of yellow avalanche lilies, similar to the pink and white curly lilies of the lowland regions. And there will be Indian paintbrush, splashes of scarlet against the grey rock, for these flowers grow anywhere on the island where it is sunny and the soil is well drained.

Finally even the flowers fade out in the thin soil and scorching sun. But life hangs on, for lichens will be found clinging to the stones, supple and growing in the wet spring, grey and brittle and barely alive during the heat of summer.

Douglas fir

In the hollows there will be snow — and even there, plants exist; sometimes the snow will be pink or even dark red, the result of a curious form of algae which thrives in snowfields.

The presence of snow profoundly affects the vegetation in the immediate vicinity, and a hiker is able to move from summer to spring to winter within a few yards as he walks towards a snowpatch. Farther away from the snow, it will be autumn, the flowers brown and withered. Closer in, there will be lines of blooms with each species blossoming at a different distance from the snow, reflecting the plant's hardiness and speed of development. Nearer yet, flowers will still be in bud — spring in August — and up tight against the snow, the shoots may not even be above the surface, although some species will poke right through the snow to get at the sun.

The presence or absence of water also profoundly affects the patterns of alpine vegetation. While some areas dry out early, others remain wet all summer, and such mountain species as marsh marigolds have learned to bloom with their feet in the water even while their heads are in the clouds. Exposure too is vital, for the wind can be as fierce as fire, burning away leaves with a freezing touch, and it blows frequently in the high country. The result is a patchwork quilt of plant life, vegetation that changes yard by yard across the hillside, forming patterns that are endlessly fascinating to those who enjoy the natural world.

The slide areas are yet another source of variety. Products of snow or rock thundering down steep slopes, preventing normal forest vegetation from forming, they lance far into the forests with their unique types of vegetation. They are pretty to look at, but are avoided by sensible people because the vegetation is composed of sinuous species such as slide alder, vine maple and devil's club, all of which present almost impossible problems for those wishing to get through them. Climbing up these thickets can be a problem, but coming down can be hazardous as well as irksome, for it is often impossible to touch the ground through the twisted branches. The hiker can find himself sliding down over the thin limbs, never quite knowing what is underneath — and if it happens to be a precipice, he can end up holding on with his hands while his feet seek desperately for the ground that is no longer there.

With the exception of a very few lowland areas (the north end of the island, the Alberni Valley, scattered patches along the west coast, and a thin strip along the east coast south of Campbell River), the island is a steep and rugged place. But the true mountain country lies north of Cowichan Lake, for the hills to the south are not tall enough to possess much alpine habitat nor steep enough to produce the rock faces and slides that characterize the mountains to the north.

Avalanche lilies

100

The colour of an alpine meadow
Top, left to right: avalanche lilies, Indian paintbrush, red and white heather; middle: Indian
paintbrush, lupin, marsh marigold; bottom: white heather and two species of lichens

Comox Glacier, where snow is the dominant feature even in mid-summer

The best alpine areas lie in Strathcona Park which straddles the center of the island west of Courtenay, for it is here that the highest mountains exist, and the park contains examples of virtually all types of Vancouver Island alpine habitat. Buttle Lake splits the park into its two main sections — the west, which is all tiny lakes and tall mountains, and the east, which boasts the twin attractions of Forbidden Plateau and the Comox glacier.

The area to the west is dominated by the two tallest mountains on Vancouver Island: Mount Elkhorn, reaching 7,190 feet, and Mount Golden Hinde, ten miles to the south, twenty-nine feet higher and lying almost in the geographic center of the island. A sharp and striking mountain, it was formerly called the Rooster Comb, for its summit is reached via a steep serrated ridge upon which climbers move with care. However, the Hinde's most arresting feature is a giant slab of stone which tilts up at an extreme angle to the northwest of the peak and was formed by geological processes which boggle the mind. It has been irreverently dubbed the Be-Hinde by island climbers.

Surrounding the Hinde is the highland lake country: to the east the grey limestone ridges of Marble Meadows and to the west a flat basin country which ultimately drains into Muchalat Inlet on the west coast. Each of these areas is dotted with small alpine lakes, often called tarns, which have a character all their own. Clear and shallow, they are bright green in the sun and steel grey in the fog, and sometimes inexplicably will be littered on the bottom with water-soaked logs which have obviously been there a long time. How long is difficult to estimate, but it is likely that decay proceeds very slowly in the alpine tarns. The source of the logs is puzzling, for the lakes are a long way from logging areas. Possibly they were dumped into the tarns by snowslides, or perhaps they are simply blow-downs accumulated over the years.

The tarns usually occur in clusters in shallow basins, one draining into another sometimes only a few feet away. The last pond often lies hard over an abyss that may be anywhere from a hundred to a thousand feet deep, the water trickling away at the outlet, suddenly to disappear over a cliff. Up high, the alpine lakes are often just pools in the rock with no nearby vegetation other than lichens and a few scattered flowers. But lower down, the tarns may be bordered by wind-battered trees, some thin and straight to shed snow and others squat and bushy to survive beneath it. All are small and widely spaced, for it is difficult to find a foothold in the meagre soil.

Lower still, the lakes exist on the upper edges of the forest, and while the trees may press close to the water in some spots, the lakes could still be classed as alpine because the trees are not the giants associated with

Alpine fir

lower regions, and the waters often nestle in stone pockets leading directly into the true alpine areas. These lakes are especially attractive, for travel is easy on the bare rocks, yet there are enough trees to provide cover. And there is likely to be good fishing as the trout have a longer growing season in warmer water and few of these lakes freeze deep enough to wipe out the fish population.

In isolated instances, even lower elevation bodies of water can be considered mountain lakes, for they are connected to the peaks by slides which have cleared away the trees almost to the water's edge. One such lake is Donner, lying at the western edge of Strathcona Park. About four miles long, it is in many ways a miniaturized version of Buttle Lake, except that it has been spared its scars. Like Buttle, Donner Lake is long and narrow, a sliver of water squeezed between Mount Colonel Foster to the north and Mount Donner to the south. The latter peak is so close to the lake that a slide falls right off it into the water, its vegetation providing a striking golden show in late autumn among the green conifers more normally found at that elevation.

Among other attractions in the western portion of Strathcona Park are the elk meadows along Tlools Creek to the north, Della Falls to the south of Buttle Lake, and the Moyeha River valley at the southwest corner of the park, an area of tall mountains and tall trees distinguished by the fact that it is the only drainage system on the continent which runs from the mountains to the sea completely within the borders of a park. While these areas are cherished by outdoorsmen, proportionately more people visit the eastern section of the park, not only because access is better, but because it includes Forbidden Plateau and the Comox glacier.

On a clear day the Comox glacier dominates the Comox valley, brooding over the mountains like a great staring white eye. It retreats in some years and grows in others, a patch of constant cold lying among stark black rocks, with Memory Lake nestled just beneath it in an austere glacial cirque overhung with heavy rock ridges, like eyebrows.

To the north lies Forbidden Plateau, for decades a favourite hiking area. Like Comox glacier, it is unique, an aberration resulting from accidents of geography. The plateau is lower than most alpine areas on Vancouver Island, and were it not for the glaciers which flattened the rock and swept the soil away, it would be thick with trees. However, it is too poorly drained to support a good forest and so exists in the margin between bog and true alpine habitat. Thin trees grow wherever they can, but through the center of Forbidden Plateau run miles of meadows, full of heather in some cases and bog plants in others, depending upon exposure and drainage. It is mainly a place of marsh marigolds and Indian paintbrush and lakes which have become famous for their fishing: Douglas and McKenzie, at the eastern end of the plateau, surrounded by hardy conifers; Panther and Kwai, connected to each other by pleasant meadows; Moat, hanging onto the edge of the plateau above Cruikshank canyon, and little tarns like those near Circlet Lake, shallow but inviting.

To the west the plateau rises, turning imperceptibly into typical island alpine habitat on the slopes of Mount Albert Edward, a world of rocks and flowers and deer trails and pink snow, where the problems of drainage are replaced by problems of soil and wind and cold typical to all the Vancouver Island mountains. Albert Edward has its own special feature, a long ridge which ends abruptly in a 3,000-foot drop off the top of the mountain.

It is a surprise, but not an atypical one; in the "little mountains" of Vancouver Island, the unusual is always over the next ridge. A person may find himself face-to-face with a mountain top that looks like a high-elevation Stonehenge — Rugged Mountain near Tahsis topped with stiff stone spires surrounding a permanent icefield; or come upon tall cliffs lined with strata, such as Mount Septimus near Della Falls; or walk along a ridge which stretches for miles, covered with open fields of flowers.

There are likely to be other surprises: a deer with its snout thrust into a bush, thrashing head and tail wildly to avoid the insects; a black bear ambling along a hillside, digging at roots; or perhaps even a wolf, lithe and black and suddenly gone, not to be seen again. It is these things that reveal the value of the mountains — places of great natural beauty that remain wilderness in the true sense of the word.

Thin, snow-shedding trees surround the meadows of the Forbidden Plateau

Overleaf/
Bear and other large mammals move into the alpine as soon as conditions permit

7/ **The Alpine Animals**

Vancouver Island marmots

When experts consider Vancouver Island's alpine animals, they think first of a mammal most people do not know even exists there — the marmot. These animals are encountered throughout North America as common woodchucks or groundhogs, but somewhat more glamorous are the alpine marmots, known as whistlers because of their call. A single sharp whistle will warn of a golden eagle drifting silently over a ridge and immediately the basin will be shrill with alarm, for alpine marmots live in colonies and usually vocalize their fear before diving into their burrows.

Four species of marmots are found in British Columbia, none out of the ordinary except for the Vancouver Island marmot which is found nowhere else in the world. Of the island's many unique varieties of mammals, only the marmot is considered by zoologists to be different enough to be designated a separate species, as distinct from other marmots as a dog from a wolf or a sockeye from a coho.

Its major difference is its colour — dark chocolate brown, quite unlike the tans and greys and silvers and whites which characterize other British Columbia varieties. (This trend towards darkness among coastal animals, known as melanism, is not confined to marmots. It is recognized in species as diverse as song sparrows, falcons and wolves, yet no one seems to know why it occurs.) The island marmot exhibits skeletal differences, but these have not been fully defined as only a very few colonies have been located. There are fears that the species is going extinct, for some previously recorded colonies are now apparently deserted, but trends cannot be established with any degree of certainty, and it is possible that more colonies will be found when an intensive search is made. Future discoveries may be difficult, however, for marmot colonies are best located by listening for their whistles while walking the island hillsides and the Vancouver Island marmot is reputed to whistle less frequently than its mainland cousin. It also hibernates seven or eight months of the year and chooses to occupy alpine meadows near the tops of tall mountains, effectively keeping out of the way of most people. Marmots have been reported from the vicinity of Jordan River to Strathcona Park, but this may simply reflect the fact that climbers are more active in these areas.

A mystery unlikely to be solved is how the marmot first reached Vancouver Island. Mountain goats, pikas and other mainland mountain species failed to move across the water barrier, but the marmots succeeded. Did they travel over some sort of land bridge during glacial times when there was more extensive alpine habitat? Were they brought by Indians? Of all the mainland animals, alpine marmots seem among the least likely candidates to have reached the island, yet they are there. And they must have been there for some time to have evolved as distinctly as they have.

Another somewhat enigmatic alpine species is the white-tailed ptarmigan. As with the marmot, few people are aware of this grouse-like bird's existence on the island, for it is more commonly associated with the far north. Its population here is not unique except for its distribution. Ptarmigans are found on relatively isolated peaks, usually over 5,000 feet, and like the marmots, their distribution is spotty. These unusually tame birds are pure white in winter and mottled brown in summer, remaining distinguishable from grouse by their white wings and tails.

The only other Vancouver Island animal found exclusively in the alpine regions is the ice worm. These worms make their homes in snow and dislike heat to such an extent that they burrow into the snowfields during the day, mainly in northfacing gullies. Small, thin and black, they can be easily mistaken for conifer needles scattered on the snow. They are common on some peaks in Strathcona Park.

Other than these three species, Vancouver Island's alpine animals are not unusual. Swifts and grey jays occur more frequently here than in the forests, and a straggler from the interior such as Clark's crow will appear every so often, but generally the mountain species are similar to those found at lower elevations. Some live in the alpine areas all year round, and the contrary blue grouse may actually migrate to alpine country for the winter, but most species are only resident when the snow is at a minimum. Big buck deer, their antlers still in velvet, will be seen

wandering high ridges; a blue grouse will be heard hooting up high in midsummer if spring is retarded that year; or a herd of elk may be encountered far up a snowslide moving over a mountain pass into the next valley.

Amphibians — frogs, toads, newts and salamanders — are probably no more numerous than in the forests, but they are often more visible in alpine areas. Their eggs may be found lying in great jellied masses at the edge of almost any body of water that lasts longer than a week or two, and later in the season, the tarns will be filled with developing tadpoles racing before the coming cold weather to complete their life-cycles.

And of course, there are insects, alpine areas seen to specialize in insects. Mosquitoes and horseflies exist in incredible numbers and while their bites are not serious, they can make midsummer life miserable for anyone unprepared. In these regions, bug repellant is often as important as lunch.

Blue grouse, hooting

A rare species of marmot found only on Vancouver Island inhabits alpine terrain similar to this

8/ The Year of the Alpine

Alpine huckleberry in autumn

The island's alpine areas are winter's domain, places where summer intrudes only briefly, and sometimes hardly at all. The one certain fact is snow, and a great deal of it.

Winter usually comes in stages in the mountains. One morning in October, perhaps even in September, the camper will awaken to find a skiff of snow on the ground, or perhaps even as much as four inches, and he will know that it is time to break camp. The first snowfall usually disappears quickly but others are sure to follow, and they do not melt away. The weather will turn bright again, for there are always good days in October, but by the end of the month the snow will be on the ground to stay, burying the autumn colours of the tough plants and converting the alpine region from a pleasant place into one where the only real concern is survival.

In some years, however, the weather remains unseasonably warm through mid-October and there are no early snowfalls. Instead, winter arrives all at once, a foot or two of snow riding a late-October storm, turning the seasons around in the space of a day. The snow from such storms does not melt but simply forms the base for more snow to come. However it arrives, by November of most years the island's peaks will be locked under three or four feet of wet, packing snow.

The differing responses of the animals to the onset of winter is a study in itself. The marmot, that most alpine of mammals, appears to live such a regulated existence that it may not even need snow to push it into hibernation; whether the weather is cold or still warm, by mid-October the island's marmots are already deep in their burrows. The onset of cooler nights also causes the amphibians to vanish, and the first frosts eliminate both the insects and many of the leafy plants. Some species of birds, too, depart long before conditions demand it, but most animals wait for the snow itself to force them down from the alpine meadows. For these species — black bear, deer, birds such as the robin, and many

The snow slumps along the gullies as water drains away

more — there is no need to anticipate the coming of winter, for in the restricted space of the island environment migrations can begin any time.

This contrasts sharply with the problem facing animals in areas where longer migrations are necessary and involve movement over tough natural barriers which must be crossed before conditions become too severe. The island animals can afford to wait until the snow begins to pile up, for they have only to head down into the valleys, and they rarely encounter serious danger.

With this type of fail-safe system, the animals can also afford to move back up the mountain as conditions permit, and they do so at most opportunities. The value of such a behaviour pattern is obvious: by remaining as high as possible, they conserve food at lower elevations for critical periods. This means that they are constantly at their survival limits and in some cases unnecessarily so since conditions do not always become truly critical. In a given winter the animals may make it somewhat more painful and difficult for themselves than necessary, but pain and difficulty are constant facts of life for mountain creatures. Survival is the only thing which really counts.

By mid-December the pattern is established: species such as deer and elk and black bears are out of the alpine areas, and species such as ptarmigan and blue grouse are hanging on just below tree-line (the ptarmigans having moved down and the grouse having moved up). The marmots and often the bears as well are locked in hibernation beneath the snow, while the fish and amphibians are lying in the mud at the bottom of lakes and ponds in a state scarcely distinguishable from death. But just as grey jays and grouse continue their normal way of life above the snow, some animals continue theirs beneath it. The voles and mice construct burrows just at the line between grass and snow, living in a weird world of diffused light, completely protected by the same snow that drives the larger animals into the forests. In spring the melting snow reveals their burrows diving in and out of the grass between holes in the sod and running for yards along the surface in a fashion that seems almost random.

As winter deepens, so does the snow. The cold descends inexorably down the mountainsides, bringing the snow lower and freezing solid the moisture-laden blanket which fell weeks before. As it falls it drifts into shapes and patterns that may remain for weeks or months . . . or, given a thaw, may be gone the next day.

The first real cold spell of winter comes as early as mid-November in some years, yet in others may never occur at all. The falling snow suddenly changes character: in place of the fluffy moisture-laden flakes of early winter come the tiny ice crystals of the truly cold periods of the

Ptarmigan

year, powder snow too dry to form a crust, lying instead on top of the old crust until the wind drives it elsewhere.

This is the period when the alpine areas show their differences most clearly. On the tall peaks and ridges the snow may not build up, for it is constantly blown away until it sifts into the forests below; but in flat, broad areas such as Forbidden Plateau the flakes have nowhere to go, and deep drifts form wherever the snow can lodge.

Interspersed with periods of intense cold are much milder periods and it is during these that the heaviest snowfalls occur, since it is usually raining below. The freezing level is critical, and if it is hovering somewhere below 5,000 feet, most of the island's alpine areas will be receiving heavy snowfalls. Every so often it rises abruptly and the low-elevation rains move right up to the peaks, soaking previously fallen snow. Such thaws are generally short-lived, but they change the entire character of the high snowfields by freezing them — which in turn means that they will persist for the entire winter.

These patterns of melt and freeze-up are sporadic, but if they occur frequently enough they will turn whole snowfields into incredible natural sculptures with cornices hanging out over space, frozen ripples like waves and tilting sheets of near-ice that will last until spring begins.

Almost imperceptibly, the final thaw comes. Bare rocks start to absorb enough energy from the sun to melt the snow around them, and rain begins to fall as frequently as snow. At first the process is scarcely distinguishable from the patterns of thaw and freeze which have gone on throughout the winter; the snow gets damp on the surface even without the help of rain, only to freeze solid again as night falls. For days the process goes on, building a crust that will support a man at night but not during the day. Sometimes the weather turns colder again for a week or two and the crust hardens even during the day, but there is a gradual warming and bit by bit, the snowpack diminishes.

With the powder snow only a memory, deer suddenly appear in ones and twos back up the hills, big antlerless bucks picking their way cautiously over passes up to 5,000 feet high, watching for soft drifts that could trap them fatally. If the weather takes a turn for the worse they wait it out, and a cold spell can even be a benefit since the snowpack may refreeze, giving them greater mobility. They don't need to worry about a snowfall that may bury them, for it isn't that time of year. So for a month or more they may walk on the snow, browsing small plants at the edge of rock faces and nipping lichens and mosses off tree trunks up to twenty feet above the ground with the help of the frozen drifts beneath them.

At this time of year a visitor to the alpine areas may not see much

Mount Golden Hinde, the island's highest peak

trace of this activity since deer leave tracks only in soft snow. But if there is a slight skiff of new flakes he will see not only deer tracks but those of squirrels and blue grouse and ptarmigan and perhaps even cougar, for all these animals become more evident with the warmth of the returning sun.

Finally, one night it does not freeze at all and the melt begins in earnest, the snow assuming new forms almost daily as it dissolves away from underneath. It begins to slump, gullies forming over each hidden rivulet, smoothing out the sharp edges until the country looks deceptively round and gentle — but it is still cold. On the alpine lakes the slumps become pockmarks and the surfaces of the lakes begin to look like the surfaces of golf balls.

The integrity of the snow is challenged in other ways. Around the margins of the lakes, tinges of blue will appear, sure signs of the coming breakup of the ice. Widening circles will be noticed about the boles of trees as the trunks add their heat to the melt, eventually leaving a foot or more of bare ground at their base while there is still two feet or more of snow nearby. And the bare patches around rocks will have expanded markedly, creating areas where real warmth can develop during the sunny days, further hastening the thaw.

Then the day arrives when the first patches of heather poke through the snow, and change accelerates as the ground is able to absorb still more heat. By this time it may be mid-July or even later, although in some years of less snow or a faster melt, the whole pattern may be shifted a month or two ahead. In such years all the plants bloom, although some, able to survive only if the ground stays moist, will die later in the dry summer. In bad years, many plants never even get a chance to push their shoots above ground as the snowpatches remain through the summer.

The uncertainty of the alpine season is reflected in the furious pace at which the plants and animals live, cramming a year of activity into much less than a normal summer. Flowers bloom quickly because they don't have much time, and blooms fade just as quickly because the plants must get on with the business of growing seeds before frost comes to nip off unfinished growth. But this cycle can be a delicate one, for a bloom formed too early is also in danger of being destroyed by cold.

Timing is everthing for the animals, too. Toads and ptarmigan alike must lay their eggs within critically short periods for the young to have a chance of survival and even then there are no guarantees; alpine weather is uncertain at best. However, like the plants, the animals here have been genetically programmed to endure the changes the seasons bring. The yearly cycles continue, always changing, but in the long term, always the same.

Red heather

Overleaf / A spelunker near the entrance to Riverbend Cavern

117

III
THE UNDERGROUND

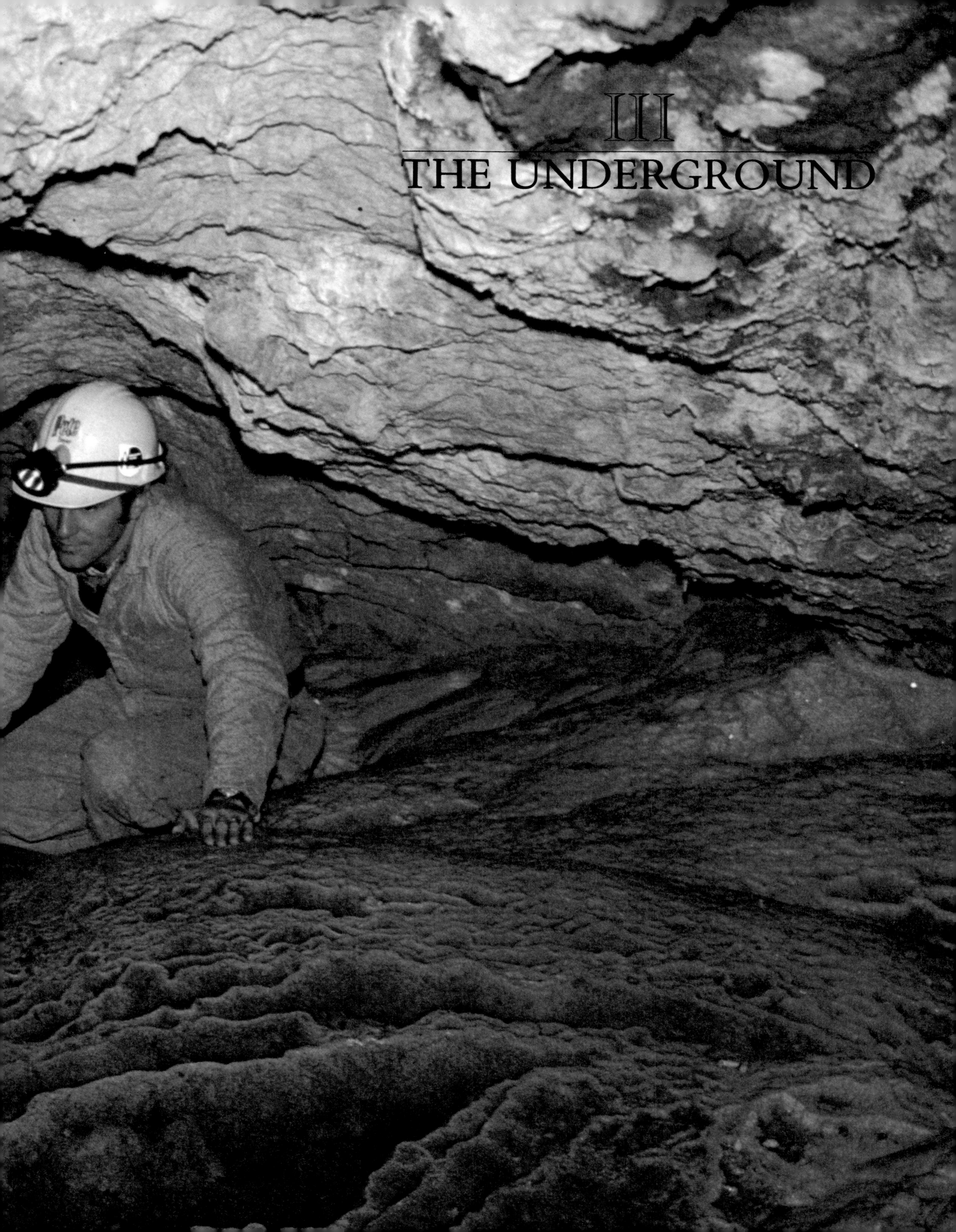

9/A World Below

Vancouver Island has its places of light — the mountain tops. It also has its places of darkness, the caves, and they are equally striking. Few people visit them, however, because their locations are not widely known and because it takes a special type of interest and equipment to explore them. But they are there, over two hundred of them catalogued so far, another of Vancouver Island's surprises. And it is estimated that there may be a cave for every five square miles of the island's surface, making a possible 2,500 in all.

A typical example is Riverbend Cavern. It was discovered west of Qualicum near Horne Lake in 1941, and then lost until 1967 when it was found again by members of the Vancouver Island Cave Exploration Group. The group's name is apt for its fifty-odd members are explorers in the true sense of the word, people in search of a frontier. The difference is that frontiers have traditionally become areas of exploitation, but the spelunkers are doing their best to preserve theirs exactly as they find it.

The original Horne Lake cave was discovered years ago and subsequently dedicated as a park. Its story has not been a happy one, however, for it has been badly damaged by vandals who have packed home pieces of the delicate limestone formations for their mantlepieces, and engaged in such senseless acts as spray-painting on the cave's walls. The damage may be repaired eventually, since the forces that built the limestone formations are still at work, but it is unlikely. Even the smallest chips take centuries to repair, and no one is prepared to estimate the length of time required to rebuild a full-sized stalagmite. Cave formations are one-shot geological creations requiring thousands upon thousands of years to evolve, but they can be destroyed in a single unfortunate instant.

Bacon strips in the Riverbend Cavern

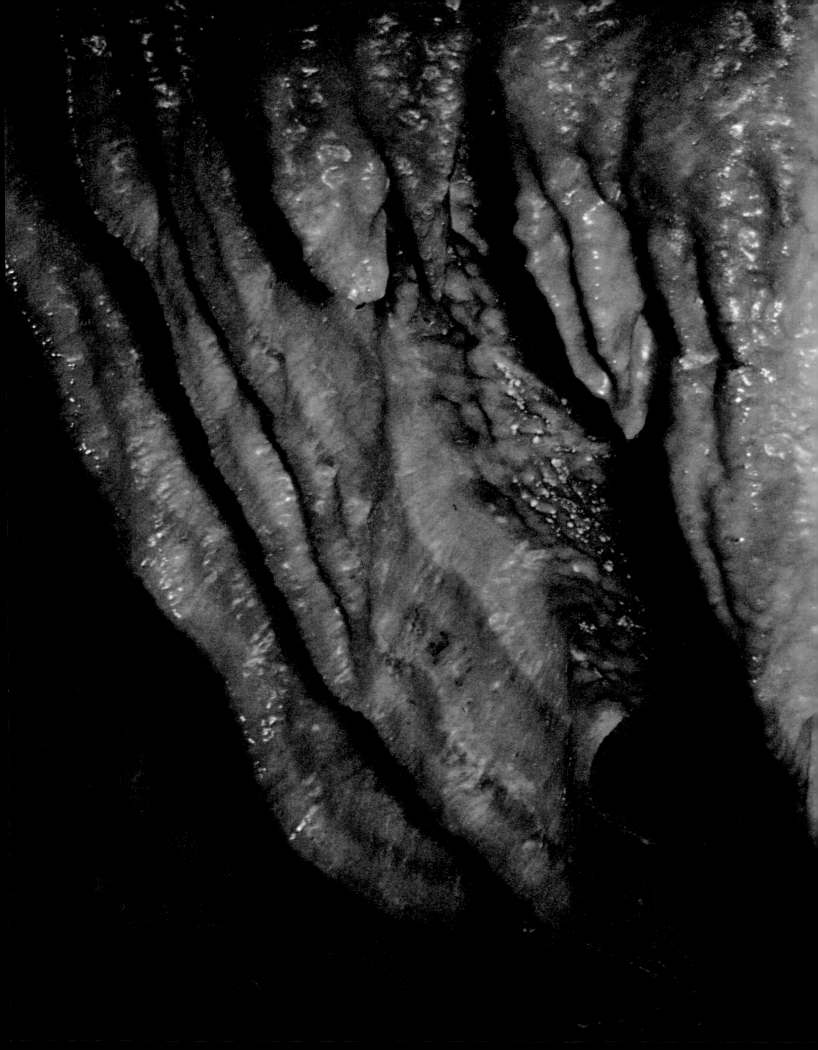

The first view of Riverbend Cavern after a pleasant hike up from the road is a big iron gate erected to block out vandals. Some damage has been done near the entrance to the cave, but it is not severe and the door should prevent any further destruction. It seems proper that the treasures of Riverbend Cavern should be locked safely away, for too many areas of Vancouver Island have been ruined forever by man and it is comforting to think that this will not be one of them.

Although every limestone cave is different, the origin of each is similar, the result of chemical action. Surface water picks up carbon dioxide on its way through the earth to form a mild carbonic acid and this works away at the limestone to form a hole in the rock far underground. Often a stream breaks through from the surface, increasing the process of cave-building by physical erosion and an underground canyon is formed, sometimes so narrow that a person can barely squeeze through it. The stream may flow through holes completely filled with water or follow a course over underground waterfalls and perhaps through underground lakes.

The ideal cave is one in which the water runs only in winter or in which some type of diversion has completely eliminated the river, allowing spelunkers access to areas that would otherwise be denied them. But this rarely happens, and water is an almost constant fact of underground life. Getting soaked in thirty-five degree pools is part of the price of cave exploration.

The hydraulic activity that spelunkers look for is the one which creates the fantastic sculptures of the underground. These are formed when limestone-bearing water trickles into the cave, dripping from the ceilings or running down the walls. If the dripping takes place slowly enough, some of the limestone settles into crystals that eventually build into recognizable structures similar to the coral reefs constructed by the patient polyps, except that in caves the beauty is all random; there is no life force required.

Although the formations may be extensive, they usually occur only at intervals with stretches of the original rock between them. The result is constant surprise: a sharp drop off into total darkness; a series of crystalline structures gleaming white and foreign in any light, or perhaps simply a blank rock wall or a pool of water so deep that it is impossible to penetrate beyond it.

Riverbend Cavern follows this pattern closely: it consists of a series of "rooms" or "galleries" linked by crawl spaces and narrow passageways. One of the largest galleries is found at the entrance and has been dubbed the "main room," as good a name as any, since it is not only large but also contains most of the types of formations found elsewhere in the cavern. There are delicate "soda straws" hanging from the ceiling — tiny hollow stalactites with water dripping through them at an almost imperceptible rate. There are halactites, odd twisted stalactites caused by drafts which prevent the slow drops of water from falling directly downward. The water leaves microscopic mineral deposits and convoluted spaghetti-like masses are formed, but they are generally just a few inches in length. And there are arrowheads, freakish stalactites resembling plumb-bobs or carrots — which explains why they are also called carrotites.

True stalactites and stalagmites are as rare in Riverbend Cavern as in most other island caves, but their absence is offset by the presence of an amazing variety of flowstone and bacon strips. Flowstone is simply a rock waterfall formed by mineral water slowly dropping over an edge or running down a wall; bacon strips are the most appropriately named formation of all, for they really do resemble giant strips of bacon, smooth or rippled, hanging from the ceiling. Even the colours are true, for while other formations tend to shades of off-white, bacon strips contain rich browns and tans.

The cave floors also have their attractions. They are often covered in flowstone broken by crystal pools — small, still bodies of water in which the crystalline processes can be clearly seen at work. If the water were running, the crystals would soon be destroyed, but the pools are absolutely still, allowing the crystals to grow slowly over the centuries. An almost unlimited assortment of other formations is found here, but perhaps the most interesting are occasional lumps of limestone resembling giant scoops of ice cream, their intricately patterned surfaces contrasting strongly with the caramel-smooth finish of the limestone in other locations.

It is this incredible variety that leads explorers down new holes in the earth, but the caves are strange places to be in. They have an almost constant temperature winter and summer and are virtually devoid of life. In Riverbend, for instance, the only life found so far is some sparse moss near the door, a bit of fungus and mould farther in and a few green flying insects which seem to have arrived by happenstance. Some caves also have spiders, in appearance like daddy-long-legs, clinging to the ceilings on spindly dark legs. One wonders what they eat and whether they are there all the time; the caves seem too sterile to support much life, yet the spiders can be quite numerous.

Larger animals occasionally make use of the caves and members of the cave exploration group have found evidence of cougar kills, but as a general rule the caves are not inhabited. Of course, that does not stop a cave explorer from wondering whether he is going to disturb something

Soda straws, Riverbend Cavern

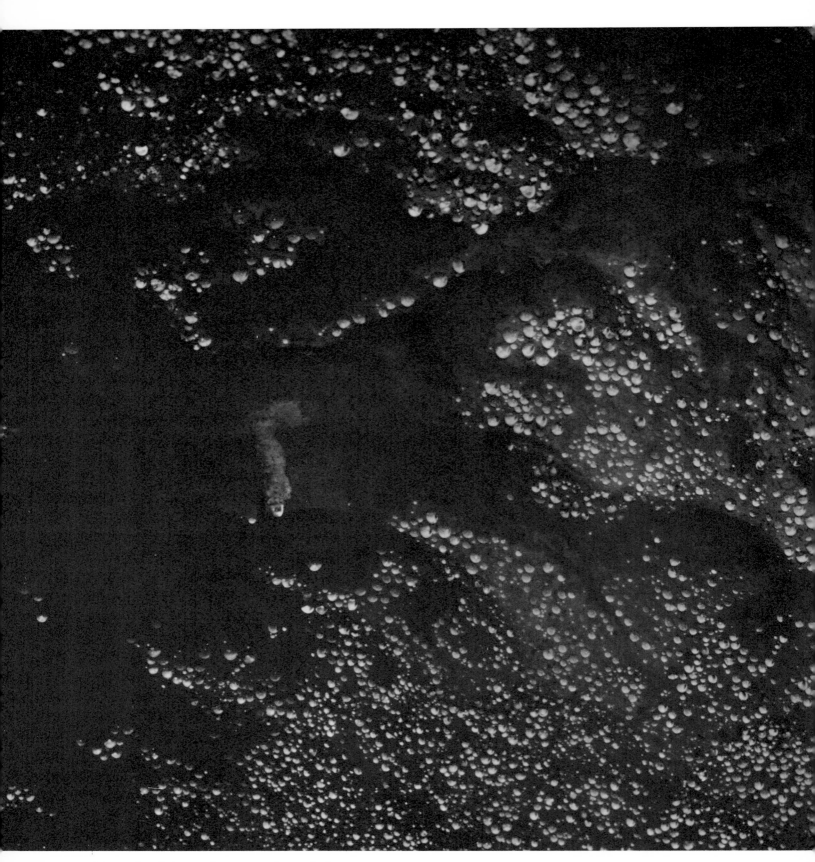

Mineralized drops of water on the roof of a cave

larger than himself each time he heads into a dark hole. But once down the ladder into Riverbend's main room, such thoughts completely disappear, for the environment would obviously be as alien to a cougar as it is to a man.

A number of chambers lead off the main room, each with different attractions. A scramble up a smooth wall to the left leads to a gallery filled with soda straws while a foray to the right reveals a minor labyrinth encased in flowstone.

But then a person must decide whether he wishes to go on, for the most difficult part of the route lies just beyond the main room. The walls and ceiling tighten in until the spelunker is forced to crawl, scuffing clothes and skin on the rough stones while trying not to damage the cave. Finally the ceiling becomes so low that it is possible to advance only by bellying along, scraping one's elbows. Then the tunnel dips and at a point known as the Siphon, a pool of water blocks the passage and there is no way to avoid it. Although the water is only about six inches deep, that is quite sufficient to provide a thorough soaking. It becomes a minor victory to succeed in keeping lunch and camera out of it.

At this point it is possible to imagine the feelings of the original explorer who had no idea whether there was anything at all beyond the Siphon; perhaps he was going to get soaked and chilled for nothing and then be forced to retreat backward after a long wet crawl. But continuing he emerged instead into one of the most beautiful caverns in the province.

Immediately following the Siphon comes a chamber which the Cave Exploration Group has titled Fleming's Folly for whimsical reasons best known to themselves. Then, after a thirty-foot vertical drop, negotiable only by rope or ladder, the spelunker reaches Achille's Pot. Here one finds rock as delicately formed as a seashell or as solid as cement, but ice-slick, where a footprint on its surface may leave a lasting stain. Or the rock may appear slippery and yet be surprisingly firm to the foot because of crystalline formations too small to be noticed. There is rock textured like brain coral and bacon strips hanging in curtains — an environment fit for gnomes, or maybe Hobbits. Experimental tapping on a sheet of stalactites which resemble organ pipes causes them to ring like crystal, each with a different tone.

Achille's Pot is also lined with flowstone and crystal pools, and from this room to the end of the cave the formations are almost continuous. A fifty-foot incline leads to the Rain Barrel where the water drips continuously, and then to the China Shop where formations sprout like albino leaves from the ceiling and walls with bacon strips and flowstone stretching off beyond the reach of lights.

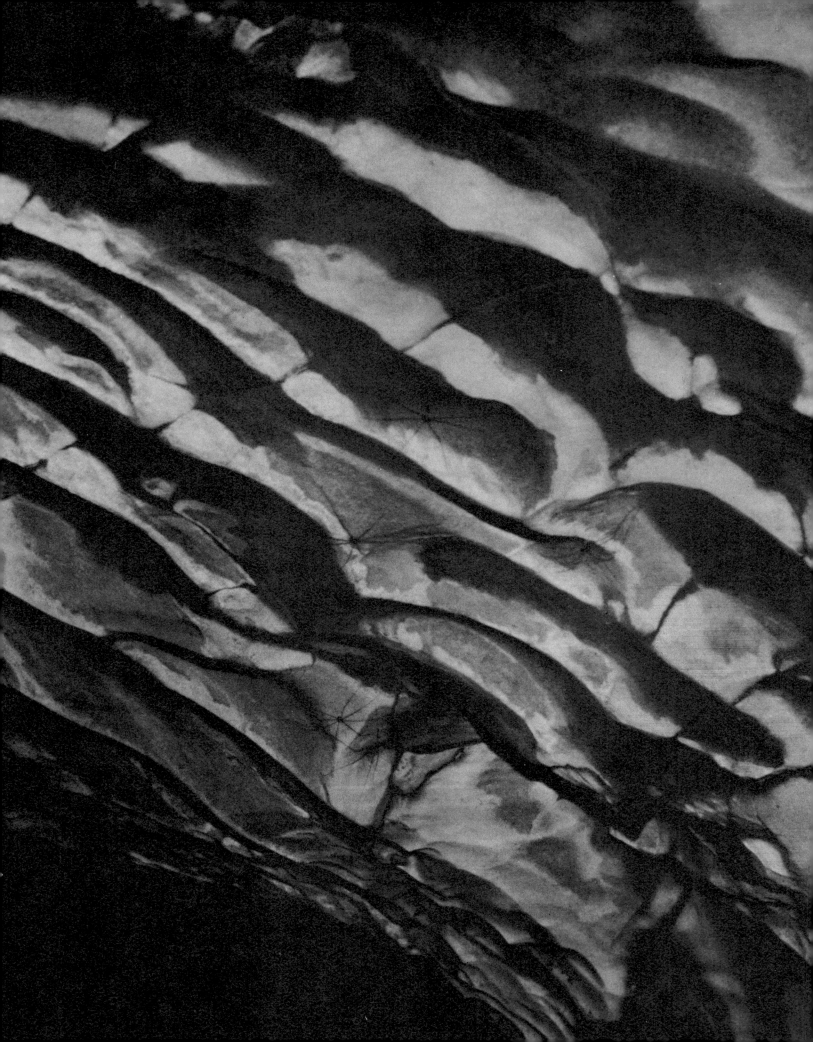

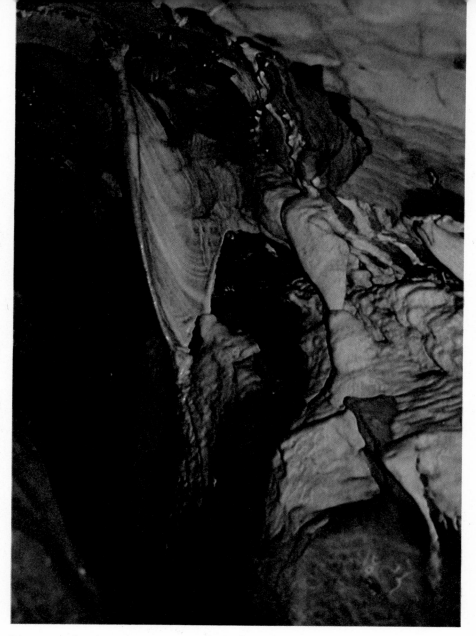

Limestone formations in a cavern along the White River

At the end, the cavern peters out in a pool of water, cutting off further exploration. It must continue, for the water goes somewhere. Perhaps just a few feet away are sights rivalling anything on earth, but more likely the river just continues underground through passages large enough for only the water itself.

The spelunkers will sit for a moment beside the final pool in River-bend Cavern, staring into the silent water and then quietly gather their gear to retrace their steps, 906 feet back and 224 feet up to the other world, the world of light.

Cave spiders on an eroded cave roof

IV
THE OCEANS

10/ Waves and Rock

The Gulf Islands in summer

Finally, irrevocably, there is the sea. The most basic fact of life on an island is the water which surrounds it, and the Vancouver Island coastline is as exciting and varied as any on earth. Like the forest, it can be divided into three general types: southeast coast, northeast coast and west coast.

Between Campbell River and Victoria lies the ocean that everyone knows, for that is where most people live, but already there have been many changes. Highways and seawalls have been constructed, estuaries have been dredged or filled and the wildlife and fish populations have diminished. It is a tribute to the enormous productivity of the area that so many ducks and salmon are still to be found.

The southeast coast is relatively free of major indentations and headlands, consisting of a series of sandy or rocky beaches occasionally backed up against cliffs. The odd river mouth or sandy spit provides variety, and the superbly scenic Gulf Islands are scattered offshore.

Some of the beaches, such as those at Parksville and on Denman Island, rival any elsewhere in Canada, for the tide goes out almost a mile over clean grey sand. Unfortunately, the waters are often too cold to make swimming pleasant and this is especially true near Victoria where an offshore upswelling generally keeps the water temperature under fifty degrees even in midsummer. Farther north, however, the tide rolls in over long stretches of sun-warmed sand or rock and the waters of the Strait of Georgia are appreciably warmer.

Previous page/
Pachena Light, one of many isolated stations along the west coast

Protected as it is by the bulk of the island, the Strait is either flat calm or rippled by nothing more annoying than a fifteen-mile per hour breeze, although occasionally a storm will keep the government ferry fleet at dockside for a few hours. Southeast Vancouver Island has a gentle, summer sort of coastline which most residents regard as their special good fortune.

The Gulf Islands are even more placid. They too have been changed by a century of farmers running sheep on the grassy headlands and loggers cutting down the trees, but they remain a mecca for those who desire the quiet life — a fine climate, pleasant scenery, and individualistic neighbours who tend to keep to themselves even if they do frequently write letters to the editor.

But this most gentle of areas was formed in fire and ice, and the evidence of volcanic action and glaciation is still clearly visible. While sandstone is the principal rock of the Gulf Islands, volcanic conglomerate is common where the lava once flowed, and giant boulders are scattered about erratically. The action of the glaciers in shaping the islands can be seen clearly from the air, for the islands have been gouged into straight lines sloping off to the southeast. The outer Gulf Islands — Gabriola, Valdes, Galiano, Mayne and Saturna — form an almost continuous barrier running out from Nanaimo towards the American side of the Strait of Georgia, providing an even more sheltered environment for islands such as Saltspring and Pender.

The Gulf Islands closely resemble the drier portions of Vancouver Island's southeast coast, with an occasional 1,000-foot hill breaking the lowland monotony on the larger islands, and they remain green through most winters. Spring transforms them into a wild garden with dozens of different wild flowers scattered about on the forest floor. The species are the same as those of the island's southeast coast forest, but they seem more prominent here because the shortage of water cuts out underbrush that would otherwise hide them from view. It also keeps the blooms in a race against drought, for entire summers sometimes pass without rain.

Because the woods are so often hot and dry, the people of the Gulf Islands turn to the beaches for relaxation, although expanses of sand are rare. Areas of pebbles separated by rocky sandstone headlands are more common and the forces of erosion have fashioned these headlands into curious formations that have become a trademark of the area. Often a kind of pock-marking leaves a stone lacework on exposed rock faces. Sometimes an undercutting action results in shallow scoops being taken out of the sandstone or, when conditions permit, true caves.

Such areas show up best on Gabriola Island near Nanaimo where they can be found in two major locations. One of these, the Malaspina Gal-

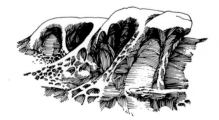

Eroded sandstone, Botanical Beach

leries, consists of a long shallow cave just above the high tide line, a ten-foot deep horizontal trench eroded out of solid rock. It lies within a provincial park, but this has not prevented the rock writers from marking the sandstone with spray paint. The results of this are rather interesting, though, since erosion occurs so fast here that the areas protected by the paint have come to stand out from the eroding rock wall.

The second area, to the south, is a 100-foot cliff, accessible only from the water. It has been drilled and channelled by wind and salt until it resembles a giant oriental puzzle. The entire cliff is a mass of eroded formations, large and small: holes in the rock only a foot or two across, set off by themselves, or great masses of sandstone eaten delicately away,

Surf rolls endlessly along the outer coasts

leaving rock lacework of striking complexity, holes behind ledges within hollows. At the tideline the cliff is extensively undermined and when the tide drops, a small boat can easily move under the overhanging edge which is bedecked with sandstone stalactites hanging from the scooped-out roof.

There is no other place quite like it on the southeast coast. The final touch is provided by seabirds nesting in the crevices and holes and in spring and summer, the cliff is alive with cormorants working to bring off their broods. They eye visitors circumspectly, but if a boatman goes about it slowly, he can edge his way underneath the nests and have a rare opportunity to watch a bird colony in action.

Eroded sandstone characteristic of the east coast

A third type of sandstone erosion is the reverse of the first two for it results not in the hollowing out of rock faces, but in the molding of sandstone boulders into curious and compelling shapes, often resembling mushrooms. Such formations are less common than the other two, but excellent examples may be found on Hornby Island.

North of Campbell River the character of the seafront begins to alter, and the hospitable southeast coast is revealed as the exception rather than the rule — a freakish accident of the unusual geography of the island.

The first hint of change occurs north of Courtenay, where a tideline may often be seen stretching into the distance across the Strait of Georgia near Mitlenatch Island. The meeting place of waters which rush in from north and south as the tide rises, it is clearly visible from the air.

The waters may sometimes boil at Mitlenatch, but the real danger lies to the north, off the southern tip of Quadra Island, at infamous Cape

The gnarled, wind-swept vegetation of the west coast can be almost impenetrable

A sea pinnacle at Bunsby Island

Mudge. This is one of the most treacherous areas on the coast for small boats: on a flood tide with a southwest wind, the seas rise with startling speed. It is here that the wide waters of the Strait of Georgia narrow to form Discovery Passage which thins in turn to the half-mile gap called Seymour Narrows, a tide-ripped channel once made more dangerous by Ripple Rock. This hazard claimed at least 120 ships and 114 lives before being eliminated by one of the largest non-nuclear blasts in world history.

The coastline of Discovery Passage serves as a suitable introduction to the northeast sea of Vancouver Island, for it is typical of the shoreline running from Campbell River to the northern tip of the island. Like the coastline to the south, it is relatively free of inlets and other irregularities and it is protected water. But the similarities stop there: the northeast coast is a more forbidding place.

The difference is due to a combination of latitude, aspect and mountains. Whereas there is a significant coastal plain to the southeast, to the north the mountains jump right out of the sea, eliminating much chance of finding beaches and shading the few that do exist. And where there is a coastal plain, as there is between Port McNeill and Port Hardy, the climate is less than inviting even in summer, for the area lies in the path of the storms which blow down the coast from Alaska.

The difference in climate is most dramatically illustrated by the vegetation which in places could only be described as ferocious. Trees crowd almost into the sea, and at the water's edge there is a dense, uninviting mat of undergrowth that at times discourages even deer. Still, the northeast coast has a fascination. It is a wilder land, with eagles wheeling in the sky and Canada geese honking in the estuaries and gulls settling like snowflakes onto log booms and islets. And there are enough fish — salmon and ling cod and herring — to support a large commercial fleet.

Perhaps the most attractive feature of the area, however, is the group of islands which lies between the mouth of Knight Inlet on the mainland coast and Port McNeill, strewn across the mouth of Johnstone Strait like flotsam. The larger islands are dark with tall conifers while the smaller ones are mere scraps of rock wearing crowns of outsize evergreens kept alive by the frequent rain.

To the west there is an even wilder shore where Queen Charlotte Strait turns to the open Pacific, a place of white sand beaches and deep inlets and rocky headlands and surf that rolls forever. This is the start of the exposed coastline, a twenty-five mile strip lying along the top end of Vancouver Island to the east of Cape Scott. The area includes some of the finest beaches in Canada, wide expanses of sand lying in shallow hollows which the sea has scooped out of the north end of the island, bearing names like Shuttleworth Bight, Nissen Bight and Nels Bight. They have not yet been discovered by most people, but they will be for they are too magnificent to remain hidden much longer. Here for the first time the Pacific breakers roll without interruption, and for those accustomed only to gentle inland waters, the effect is dramatic: combers that never stop roaring as they batter themselves to white froth against the cold sand.

The headlands, too, are a source of wonder for those who have never stood before an open ocean. The sea hits in myriad ways according to the configuration of the rock. Sometimes the spray is flung high, a hundred feet or more in a storm; in other spots, the waves perish in surges, foaming white fingers seething up the rocks twenty feet or more, only to dribble back before the next wave sends them swelling upward again. In still other places, the waves rush through narrow vertical gaps in the rock, forming blowholes, the spray shooting straight up as if from a hose.

Rock pinnacle

The life of a tide pool
Top, left to right: starfish, sea urchins, starfish; middle: sea palms, limpets, sea anemone;
bottom: a tide pool at Botanical Beach

138

The rugged northwest coast in winter

Amid this confusion live the plants and animals of the shoreline, clinging desperately to the rocks before forces that break down continents. Some are solid as the stones themselves and some are supple, presenting no resistance to the waves but holding on with fierce intensity.

Seaweeds as varied as forest plants grow here, ranging in size from giant kelp which lies in beds offshore to barely visible algaes. Kelp is the most noticeable species, distinguished by a long slender stem held upright by a hollow bulbous top and tied down by a holdfast which looks like a root system but which is only a very efficient anchor. Long brown fronds resembling flexible leaves sprout from the bulb, which may be as much as thirty to fifty feet from the holdfast.

Even more interesting in appearance is a curious seaweed known as a sea palm. Less than a foot high, it has a strong but flexible "trunk" that stands upright when the tide has left it dry (which is not often, for it exists close to the low tide mark), but which readily bends before the

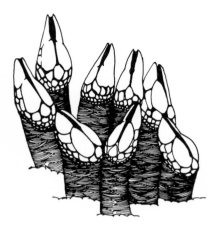

Goose barnacles

battering waves. Atop the trunk are small "leaves" like those of a miniature palm tree.

Many varieties of algae abound, sometimes green and purple but more often brown. They grow furiously in summer and break off in winter storms to end up in wind-rows along the beaches, sometimes heaped two or three feet high — fantastic fertilizer if only there were some way to move it off the beach.

While the seaweeds survive largely by being flexible, most animals of the headlands manage to exist only by emulating rocks. Supple, plant-like animals such as sea anemones live in the waves, but the most common defense against the pounding water is heavy armour — a shell of great strength — and a very secure holdfast. Mussels, barnacles and other molluscs are often present in great profusion and they reach formidable size — up to ten inches for one species of mussel and almost half a foot across for the biggest barnacles.

Tidepools, while common to all beaches, reach their greatest diversity and beauty along the rocky headlands of the island's outer coast where they occur in great variety according to differences in the rock, their degree of exposure to the waves and their relative level in the intertidal zone.

Some tidepools actually occur above the high tide mark and are brackish mixtures of rainwater and spray that usually support little except minute slimy algae. But even these uninviting pools can be interesting where cleavage patterns in the rock have produced odd, sharp geometric shapes.

A few feet lower the waves get a chance to work, freshening the waters of the tidepools daily even if only for an hour or so at high tide. This results in a much greater variety of sealife, but it is still a tough place to exist, too hot in summer and perhaps too cold in winter. Only the hardiest of the intertidal creatures manage to survive in these pools — tiny snails, bullheads (a small fish of the sculpin family) and limpets (molluscs with a shell shaped like the conical hat of an Oriental rice farmer), all existing amid soft gardens of seaweed.

Lower still in the tide zone, the pools generally become wider and deeper, allowing more types of animals and plants to exist because there is better buffering against extremes of temperature and because the pools are washed more often by the surf, giving a better food supply. It is here that starfish and sea urchins and sea anemones are found.

Starfish come in a range of shapes and colours; most are sluggish, a few are not. The most common variety is a rugged, five-armed purple specimen about a foot in diameter. Its most interesting feature is that if chopped up, it will often grow a new body onto the various pieces, providing they are big enough. For all its lethargic ways, like most sea creatures it is a fierce predator and once it envelops a clam, it rarely lets go. It grabs both sides of the shellfish with hundreds of tiny suction-cup feet, exerting a steady killing pressure which eventually forces the clam to open up; then the starfish everts its stomach to digest the clam inside out, a startling procedure for those unfamiliar with it.

Other types of starfish may also be seen: bright red, very stiff creatures, five inches across; many-armed, soft sun-stars, two feet or more in diameter; brittle stars with five slender, flexible legs poking from under a hard central body, legs which wave frantically if the animal is disturbed under a rock. On rare occasions, a tidepool will contain a misplaced basket star, the strangest species of them all. It is a deep water form, pure white and brittle, with arms that repeatedly branch until they resemble the sides of a wicker basket perhaps a foot and a half wide.

Waves roll in from two directions at Cape Scott

Sea urchins, shelled, spiny creatures which look like pincushions, also fascinate tidepool observers. Most common is a small green specimen up to four inches in diameter with spines less than an inch long, but there is also a purple variety which grows at least twice that size. When sea urchins die, the spines drop off to reveal a delicate patterned shell.

Closely related to sea urchins but quite different in appearance are sand dollars — round and flat and smooth and gray. They are beach rather than headland creatures and may cover acres of sand at the low tide mark, so densely packed that it is impossible to walk without stepping on them.

Sea anemones are completely different — so different, in fact, that they are often mistaken for plants. They are the simplest kind of animal: tentacles to grab food, a mouth to receive it and a stomach to absorb it. They clutch the rocks on suction-cup bases, waiting with their stinging tentacles for unwary fish to pass. The stings are deadly to many aquatic animals, but they are of little consequence to humans. The most common species of sea anemone (again, like the sea urchin, small and green) is often poked by children for the simple fun of watching the animal attempting to swallow a finger.

The most interesting tidepools lie at the bottom of the tide zone where they are exposed to the air for only a short time during the lowest tides of the year. These pools exhibit a sample of the habitat usually seen only by the scuba diver — large sea urchins, unusual starfish and sea anemones and perhaps even an octopus or a large fish. There may also be abalones, among the tastiest and prettiest shellfish on the coast with shells of mother-of-pearl distinguished by a row of holes down the edge. In these pools there is an almost unbelievable blanket of sea life, sponges piled on mussels growing on barnacles clinging to rock with seaweed intertwined.

Ornamented with sea life and tortured rock, the exposed headlands are places of wide appeal and the most exposed of all is Cape Scott. It is often referred to as the northernmost point of Vancouver Island, but in fact it is not, since the flat top end of the island tilts slightly to the northeast. The northernmost point turns out to be Cape Sutil, some twenty miles east, leaving Cape Scott as the westernmost point. It is really just a small hill, a piece of rock containing a forest and a lighthouse, connected to Vancouver Island by a thin isthmus of sand which has the unusual distinction of being battered simultaneously by open ocean waves from both north and south. The result is a bizzare formation that looks like two beaches placed back to back with sand dunes in the center. In sunlight, it springs into sharp relief: blue waters, white sand and even whiter surf. It is the last of the island's west coast beaches and in many ways, the most spectacular, a place of raging weather and great beauty.

A black sand beach near Kyoquot

Wave patterns in the sand at Pachena Bay

The area has other attractions. Offshore lie the Scott islands while just behind the cape lies Hansen Lagoon, the northernmost of the island's many inlets and one of its most curious. Hansen Lagoon is about four miles long and when the tide goes out, the entire four-mile inlet is transformed into a giant mud flat, drawing ducks and geese by the thousands. Although the lagoon does not go completely dry, it does become shallow enough that pilots refuse to land planes there except at high tide.

At the head of the lagoon is the wide estuary of the Fisherman River which has attracted waves of settlers since the 1890s, only to crush each in turn with distance and weather: it is marginal farming land at best, and the problem of marketing its produce has never been satisfactorily solved. A few hardy souls still live in the vicinity, but it is not the sort of country where a family can build for the future. At the north end of Vancouver Island, the future has always meant escape to more civilized climes.

South of Cape Scott the seacoast changes again, becoming a fascinating mixture of beaches, peninsulas, inlets and islands which so far has withstood man's assaults remarkably well. While mariners divide the coastline by its promontories — Cape Cook, Estevan Point and Cape Beale — the small boat fraternity think in terms of the major inlets since they provide convenient routes to areas otherwise inaccessible. The inlets poke sinuous saltwater fingers deep into the mountains and forests, and their names — Indian, Spanish, Scandinavian and English — suggest the role that they have played in the island's history.

Out from the inlets lie islands which range in size from giants like Nootka and Flores down to tiny chunks of rock almost submerged at high tide. While the bigger islands are not significantly different from the rest of the coast, the smaller ones have a special character. Those that are sheltered in the mouths of the inlets resemble the islands along the northeast coast, but the most spectacular islands lie offshore where the wind and waves can get at them, carving vegetation and rock into wild forms. The effect is one of static force, a sort of dynamic equilibrium involving the power of wind and surf, and the power of the trees and bushes growing in the face of such adversity. There is everywhere evidence of violent action — broken snags and broken rocks and howling storms. Perhaps there is a freighter lying bent and broken on the shore — and just as a ship can die in a day of such weather, so it would seem that the islands must change daily under the onslaught. But it is not so. A year later, the grounded freighter may be nearly gone, shattered by winter storms, but the rocks and the trees and even the bushes will be unchanged. The same rock arch, seemingly as delicate as crystal, will be still standing, and the same dead tree will still be clutching

The wreck of the "Vanlene"

Wherever there are cracks in the rock, the sea finds a way in

its eagle nest in gaunt and broken limbs. The fragile east coast sandstone erodes yearly, but the west coast rock endures for centuries because anything soft in it has long since worn away.

There are islands scattered along the length of the west coast, but in three areas they dominate the seascape — near Kyoquot, north of Tofino and in Barkley Sound. The latter group, known as the Effingham Islands, stand out. Ripped by wind and laced with curious rock formations, they cover about forty square miles at the entrance to Barkley Sound where they represent a major hazard to large ships and a major delight to small boaters who can ply the channels in relative safety providing they pick their weather conditions. On a sparkling day, the Effingham Islands are a sight not soon forgotten, and in a storm they are even more magnificent, wind whipped trees and white water all around. The outer islands are the most exposed, and these are chosen by sea lions as rookeries, while the inner islands contain one of the densest nesting populations of bald eagles on the coast.

Whyac, an Indian village at Nitinat Narrows

In sharp contrast to the islands are the beaches, strung between the headlands up and down the west coast. They may be narrow or wide, flat or sharply sloping, with white sand or black, fine sand or coarse — but wherever they occur, they dominate.

The finest of all west coast beaches is Long Beach — such a magnificent stretch of sand that it was feared that the Japanese might use it as a landing area during World War II. Accordingly, preventive rows of posts were erected between the tide lines at this and other nearby beaches where they stood for years, encrusted with sea life. But of course they were never needed, for the Japanese never landed.

Occasionally other evidence of the war such as life rafts drifted ashore, sometimes complete with provisions. Now the flotsam and jetsom comprise only items of peaceful maritime activity, often inscribed with Japanese or Russian characters, for a cosmopolitan fishing fleet operates off the coast these days. Aficionados spend hours walking the sand, searching for the most prized items that wash ashore: glass fishing floats, some shaped like rolling pins, others as large as a foot and a half in diameter. The experts learn to arrive on the beach right after storms and find that it pays to peer under driftwood and even up in the bushes, for floats can be tossed high by the surf.

At Long Beach cars now seem as common as seagulls, but there are many other beaches along this coast that may be even more deserted than they were 150 years ago, for most of their Indian inhabitants have left. Two of the finest occur on Vargas and Flores Islands north of Tofino, but there are others, particularly near Brooks Peninsula.

Long stretches of sand predominate on these beaches, but there are other attractions. There may be a river running sluggishly down to the shore, then meandering parallel to the waves for hundreds of yards before finally breaking through the sand to meet the sea. Such streams are usually tidal in their lower reaches, running at low water but filling again from the ocean as the tide returns.

A visitor to the west coast's beaches is always struck by the immense quantity of driftwood — twisted roots clawing at the sky or logs broken and slivered into forms like giant woolly caterpillars, their surfaces smashed and rough from the pounding of the waves. The wood piles up in windrows like great grey bones along the shore, a splintered surrealistic seascape created by logging activity.

Where wind and sand conditions are right, there may be sand dunes, but the most compelling feature of these beaches is the vegetation. At exposed locations it consists of an unbroken mat sloping up and away from the wind — thick salal melding with spruce and salmonberry and cedar to form a solid wall which the wind cannot penetrate but under which nothing can grow because of the absence of light. Out of this living mat burst evergreens, mainly spruce and cedar which, like the shrubs, are bent away from the gales. They will have had branches burnt in the cold spray but will nevertheless endure.

In a few scattered and forgotten locations along the west coast, the thick seaside shrubs may conceal the rotting remains of ancient Indian villages. For 4000 years or more the west coast Indians lived a life in rhythm with the sea, digging shellfish and gathering berries and harpooning salmon and sometimes, whales. The interior of the island was well known to them, but they chose not to live there for the easy life was on the coast where the temperatures were milder and food was more readily available.

Totem, Pachena Bay

Sometimes they died from red tide — paralytic shellfish poisoning — sometimes they died in inter-village skirmishes, and a few were slaves, but mostly the life was good. With unerring judgment, they chose the best spots for their villages, places that could be defended easily with good views of the sea so that enemies could not take them unaware, but places which were as sheltered as possible from the inevitable wind. A visitor can still stand at the old sites and watch waves lap almost motionlessly against a gentle beach while outside, a scant hundred yards away, the seas are boiling.

Now the villages are almost gone and in some spots, only a level piece of ground indicates that people once lived there. Sometimes a decaying totem pole will poke out of the bushes, displaying a crown of salal, for the living forest cannot leave a potential growing site untouched.

In the underbrush nearby there may be other remains: the foundations of a house festooned with thick moss, or a fallen totem lying under the roots of a giant spruce. And trees may have grown from the top of house-posts, completely splitting them as the roots worked down through the wood to the forest floor. In the forest, there may be a half-finished dugout canoe, waiting for a carver who never returned. Now, a hundred years later, the shape is still discernible but the moss is deep on the rotting wood and the wood will soon be gone.

The story of the west coast is not all one of abandonment, however, for some of the ancient villages are still occupied. Children play beneath totems at spots like Alert Bay and Friendly Cove, and fishermen tie up at pretty villages like Ahousat and Kyoquot; but the settlements have changed. A totem may still stand overlooking the beach, but the big plank houses have been replaced by frame structures, and the men work from fishboats rather than dugouts, and no one hunts the whales any more.

Totems lie rotting under the quickly regenerating forest

It is small wonder that people grow to love the west coast, and among its more fascinating aspects are areas of rock which have been beaten by the elements into strange and wonderful shapes. Sea caves dot the coast, stretching like crooked tongues into clefts in the rock near the tide line, fifty feet deep or more. Many contain water at all times and are inaccessible. Even scuba divers are taking great risks if they explore such territory, for the surging waves pack tremendous power and can rip off facemasks and other gear. Some sea caves are now a distance inland and are always dry as a result of geological forces which have lifted the land above the high tide line. These are generally found at the end of long gullies near the beach, their entrances often hidden by the thick west coast vegetation. Occasionally such a cave will contain Indian remains, for the coastal tribes used caves as burial places. There may be masks or cedar blankets near the casket, but they should be left strictly alone. It is illegal to disturb burial caves.

If the waves break through the far side of a cave, an arch will be formed. One of the best examples lies on a small island at the entrance to Esperanza Inlet, south of Brooks Peninsula; but the most famous is Hole-in-the-Wall just north of Nitinat Lake, visible for miles in both directions.

Another surprise are the stone pillars which have been rounded by the sea but which remain too tough to be broken. Almost every headland boasts some sort of pillar — one at the south side of Pachena Bay is of particular interest because it has been hollowed out at its base, forming a cave within a pillar.

Also of interest are the great rock shelves which stretch out for hundreds of feet in the intertidal zone at numerous points along the west coast. These shelves often occur at the base of cliffs and can prove hazardous for hikers since they may be completely covered at high tide, leaving no place for escape. They can be fascinating to visit, if one is cautious, because the various tidal life zones are spread out vertically along them. Tidal creatures are compressed into distinct layers according to the amount of time they can spend out of the water, and these layers are usually only a few feet wide. On the shelves, however, a particular layer may stretch over a tenth of a mile because the shelf drops away very slowly. At one location there may be fields of one type of seaweed while mussels will cover acres of rock at another, and yet a different type of seaweed may dominate elsewhere.

The shelves often have another totally unexpected feature — tiny ridges of rock, usually only an inch or two high, which have resulted from harder strata being left intact while the softer rock has eroded away around them. In some places these strata have been broken and shifted by earthquakes so that faults in the rock are clearly delineated.

Beyond these rock shelves, the sea bottom often slopes only very gradually, permitting enormous undersea forests of kelp to develop.

Other surprises include a hot spring just north of Flores Island and a reversing falls at the entrance to Johnson Lagoon just south of Brooks Peninsula. The lagoon entrance is so narrow that as the tide drops, the water cannot run out fast enough so that eventually it is higher inside the lagoon than outside, forming a waterfall. When the tide changes the situation reverses itself. And there is Lawn Point, a curious spit which pokes out into the Pacific just south of Quatsino Sound. Trees cannot grow here because of the unmerciful wind and thus Lawn Point gets its name, for it contains only grass and low bushes — a welcome grazing area for deer. Even the sand has its oddities: in places, it squeaks underfoot which has led to at least one resort being called "Singing Sands."

Perhaps the west coast's most unusual features are the giant landmark peninsulas, Hesquiat and Brooks, both over ten miles long and about six miles wide. Hesquiat Peninsula is flat and swampy, while Brooks Peninsula's cloud-draped mountains seem strange and foreign even though they are clearly continuations of the mountains which run out from the center of the island and which dominate the west coast. It seems incongruous to find peaks of over 2,000 feet eight miles out at sea. Mariners have learned to beware of both peninsulas not just because they project far out to sea but because of hazardous flat rocky shelves running underwater hundreds of yards offshore.

A third major jut of land, Cape Beale, is far less impressive in size but offers a series of small scooped beaches along its northern and western sides. Like Hesquiat Peninsula, Cape Beale has extensive inland marshes and like many other areas of the coast, it is rich in Indian history. The remains of Indian villages lie in the thick salal with an occasional giant centerpost still visible on the ground, and visitors seek out Execution Rock where Nootka villagers once hurled captives to their deaths off a frightening cliff.

Between Cape Beale and Sooke, there are only three possible harbours — Pachena Bay, Nitinat Lake and Port San Juan — and of these, only two are really safe. The run into Nitinat Lake involves crossing through Nitinat Narrows and over Nitinat Bar, and even whales become stranded here. But for all its dangers, this section of the coast is a place of great beauty. There are fine beaches at spots like Pachena Bay and Clo-oose, and the high incidence of sandstone cliffs with waterfalls dropping onto the beaches below makes the area quite unique.

This portion of the coastline is fast becoming one of the major recreational areas of the island as increasing numbers of backpackers hike the west coast trail between Pachena Bay and Port Renfrew, but it was once

Pilots call the area near Knight Inlet "the thousand islands"

a disaster area. The trail was originally hacked out of the west coast jungle because shipwrecks were so common that the area between Cape Beale and Port Renfrew had become known as the "graveyard of the Pacific." Before the trail was established, it was extremely difficult to reach ships that went aground, and survivors who managed to get to shore faced staggering hardships in reaching civilization. It still is not easy, but the trail, completed in 1908, has been a major assistance to the survivors of wrecks.

To further aid mariners, the government erected a string of lighthouses along the west coast at convenient headlands, and they became as much a part of the coast as the beaches and the twisted trees. But their end is near, for the lighthouses are being phased out, one by one.

Like all the sections of the island's outer coast, the area south of Cape Beale has its special attractions. The beaches tend to be golden rather than white, and more sharply sloping. And Breakwater Beach just north of Carmanah Point is unlike any other on the island, for it possesses a natural breakwater of black basalt, curving out from a point to enclose a fine stretch of sand that goes completely dry when the tide retreats. This area also includes the Hole-in-the-Wall arch and beautiful Tsusiat Falls. Each mile of shoreline here brings its own unique formations: smooth expanses of cliff or rock hollowed out like a giant punchbowl, such as the one at Owen Point, or offshore rocks like battleships. And this is the country of sea caves; the area between Port Renfrew and Jordan River is riddled with them, the most accessible being near Sombrio Point.

In this area, too, the sea begins to tame, for the shore is protected by Cape Flattery across the Strait of Juan de Fuca on the American shore. The combers start to flatten out, surging into life only during a storm, and the gentle southeast coast is only a few miles away, bathed in sunshine instead of wind.

Race Rocks lighthouse

153

11/ Inlets and Estuaries

To most people, the west coast of Vancouver Island evokes images of beaches and shipwrecks and sea lions, a place of wild scenery where water is never still. But the island also has a gentle side, provided by the many inlets which link the surf and the forests — meandering waterways which in two cases stretch better than halfway across the island. Except for their salty water and tides, they could pass for lakes, and they present a striking contrast to the rugged conditions which prevail on the open coast. Inlets are usually spared both the fogs which so often roll in over the outer beaches on a hot day and the swells of the open ocean, and they would be ideal for small boat exploration were it not for the wind which often whips up dangerous waves as it is funneled between the hills.

For years, the only truly accessible inlet was the Alberni Canal. It took people a long time to realize the recreational potential that it represented — time, and the development of boats and motors suitable for use in such an area. At first, the canal was valued as a water highway, an easy route for freighters and commercial fishermen from the open ocean to the city of Alberni. Local anglers enjoyed fishing for the giant tyee salmon which in late summer gathered at the mouth of the Somass River near the head of the inlet. But it was not until after World War II that people really started to sample the inlet's attractions. Tourists began to use its ferry service as a convenient method of reaching Long Beach, and small boaters ventured farther afield, exploring places like the Effingham Islands. They also discovered the tyee run at Nahmint which became the inlet's primary salmon spot after fishing declined at the mouth of the Somass River. Today, the Alberni Inlet is heavily used by recreationists (there is scarcely a beach without campers in Barkley Sound in mid-summer), but surprisingly few have bothered to look for similar areas elsewhere.

Trumpeter swan

The retreating tide near Tofino leaves an ideal wildlife refuge

However, north of Alberni Inlet lies a labyrinth of waterways snaking into the mountains and all have suddenly become accessible, for as the loggers tamed one wilderness, they opened the way to another, providing new routes to the surf of the Pacific. In area after area, they have recently broken through the mountain divides to join up with long-standing logging shows at the heads of the west coast inlets, and now the fiords provide easy avenues to surprisingly distant areas of Vancouver Island's coastline.

Port Renfrew, Bamfield, Ucluelet, Tofino, Gold River, Tahsis, Zeballos, Fair Harbor, Holberg, Coal Harbor, Port Alice, Winter Harbor: one by one, from the bottom of the island to the top, the tiny west coast communities have been linked to the rest of the island. The roads may be bumpy and narrow and often closed, but they are there.

While inlets such as Quatsino Sound lie in fairly flat country, most are squeezed between tall walls of rock, prickly with conifers. The forest along the shores is often broken by rock outcroppings and sometimes the bluffs turn into cliffs which jut awesomely over the boats below. The scenery alters constantly under the influence of sunshine and cloud and wind, changing with each hour and with each bend in the shore-line. Sometimes fog will move in and the boater will be forced to inch

A creek finally breaks through to the sea

along the coast, watching intently for rocks; at other times the clouds will roll away, revealing spectacular stretches of coast backed by snowy peaks. Suddenly, a sixty-pound salmon will roll with a splash, or a seal will poke its head out of the ripples, or a pod of killer whales will be all around the boat, and one wonders what the next mile will bring.

The inlets come in all shapes and sizes: Quatsino Sound, composed of three inlets running haphazardly in all directions and bearing the dubious distinction of being among the most polluted of the island's west coast waterways; Nootka Sound, whose inlets resemble a three-fingered hand; Kyoquot Sound, site of Fair Harbor, a town distinguished by the fact that as soon as the road reached it, all the people left; and the inlets near Tofino, shorter and less twisted than the island's other fiords.

But it is not necessary to travel to the west coast to see a Vancouver Island inlet. One of the largest lies along the Island Highway not far from Victoria, and those driving the Malahat get a superb view of it from above. This is Saanich Inlet, an eighteen-mile gash which separates the strawberry fields of Saanich from the rest of the island. Aside from the fact that it empties into the gentle Gulf of Georgia rather than into the open swells of the Pacific Ocean, it is a typical island fiord. Lying between good-sized hills, it is fed by numerous rivers and creeks and contains a flat and fertile estuary at its head.

To many people, the estuary is the most interesting feature of an inlet for that is where it all begins — where the river meets the sea, where fresh water meets salt. From above, an estuary is always clearly discernible, a level plain ending in a fan-shaped delta where river sediments spill into the ocean, a place of mud and swamp grasses laced by channels in which the waters rise and fall with the tides. The grasses provide a sharp colour contrast to the surrounding conifers, turning from a golden brown in late summer to a brilliant green as the fresh shoots sprout in early spring.

But the real contrast is in the soil which is extremely rich since it receives nutrients leached out of the forest slopes upstream. The fertility of the soil makes estuaries among the most productive and valuable lands on earth with an importance out of all proportion to their size. At estuaries, young salmon acclimatize themselves to the ocean after emerging from the fresh water and gather there again near the end of their lives to make a final run at the river. And it is here that many species of waterfowl raise their broods, and where almost all ducks and geese and swans and shorebirds spend a good portion of the winter and spring. During the coldest periods of winter, the estuaries are particularly important to waterfowl on Vancouver Island as ponds and lakes become frozen and unavailable.

Canada goose

Overleaf/

Tlupana Inlet, just one of many fiords along the west coast north of Tofino   157

While the island's estuaries are similar to each other in pattern, they are quite different in size and in some instances, almost an entire inlet could be termed an estuary. Hansen Lagoon is one example, but perhaps the best known of these areas lies in the backwaters south of Tofino behind Long Beach. Here the tide drops to reveal mile after mile of mud. The result is a naturalist's paradise: ducks and geese by the thousands at migration; seals, sea lions, racoons and otters; eagles, ospreys and dozens of types of shorebirds as well as fish, oysters and clams.

Hansen Lagoon and the Tofino mud flats are exceptions, however, for most of the island's estuaries are much smaller — and being smaller, are far more vulnerable to destruction. They have become the natural focus of man's activity and it will take more careful planning to protect them from the abuses which have been common in the past.

The island's largest concentration of trumpeter swans occurs at the estuary of the Somass River at Port Alberni

12/ **Where No Trees Grow**

*The wind eliminates the forest
as most people know it at
Brooks Peninsula*

The effects of rain are apparent enough on Vancouver Island, but it is only in the alpine areas and near the coast that the effects of wind become noticeable. And just as the west coast receives the bulk of the rainfall, so it also receives much more than its share of wind. All along the open shores, the vegetation is molded by the storms, producing a tangled and virtually impenetrable wall of undergrowth, bush piled upon bush, each struggling to find shelter.

In a very few locations, however, the wind is too strong for vegetation to resist, and at Brooks Peninsula the ocean gales achieve an ultimate victory — the elimination of the forest as most people know it.

Brooks Peninsula is an odd area near the north end of Vancouver Island, a chunky peninsula six miles wide which juts out ten miles into the open Pacific where it catches the full force of the winds that sweep in from both north and west. It is a place of fierce storms and heavy salt spray, and the result on the forest is startling. In places no trees can grow and the country has come to resemble a bog, although some people would argue that it is really a form of alpine habitat or perhaps a moor. Whatever the designation, it is a fact that on parts of Brooks Peninsula, alpine-like vegetation begins not more than two hundred yards from the beach, and the stunted pines and grasses and ponds typical of bog country are found. These can be a bonanza for deer who usually have to scrape to find food along the west coast.

Brooks Peninsula is rugged, but there are places where conditions are even tougher. One such spot is Triangle Island which lies about thirty miles off the extreme northwest corner of Vancouver Island, a place so far away that most maps of the area do not even bother to include it. The only reason it is associated with Vancouver Island at all is that there is no other land even close to it.

Bonsai hemlock in a bog

160

Triangle Island is an area of unique geography and incredible storms, a place where the weather is so severe that trees cannot grow at all, yet a place where seabirds and marine mammals thrive in numbers which have made it famous among naturalists. As the name implies, the island is roughly three-sided with peninsulas of tortured stone jutting out at each corner to hold the sand in place. These headlands have been eroded into spectacular caves and arches and pinnacles, but they are easily over-shadowed by the odd angular shape of the island itself. It is all flat planes and corners, almost like a rough-cut crystal, except that it is covered by grass and bush which contrasts sharply with the stark rocks below. The landscape is made even more alien by the presence of jagged chunks of rock offshore, black and forbidding in the heaving sea.

Triangle Island is about 400 feet above sea level at its highest point, and there was once a light station there. It was abandoned after the wind blew down one of the buildings, but not, rumour has it, until at least one light keeper went mad with loneliness and fear. That is not unusual on this desolate coast.

Triangle Island is among the more forbidding spots on the coast, but it is also one of the prettiest when the weather is good. The hillsides are covered with bushes, herbaceous plants and tussock grasses quite unlike the grasses found in places with a more hospitable climate. Vegetation lies brown and dormant in the cooler months but, like the estuaries, Triangle Island turns brilliant green in spring when it vibrates with life.

The greening of the island coincides with the breeding of the seabirds and in most places, every tussock of grass seems to cover a nest hole. Burrows riddle the soft earth, rendering it spongy to walk on and leaving the indelible impression of an abundance of life. There will be bald eagles in the sky and sea lions by the hundreds on the rocks below. Sea-birds will dart past like bullets, perhaps with a falcon in close pursuit, and offshore a pod of grey whales may be loafing just out from the beach, apparently oblivious to the activity about them.

At first viewing, Triangle Island appears to be unique, a one-shot creation, but it is actually one of three such islands off Cape Scott: Beresford and Sartine islands are fully as interesting if considerably smaller. Together with two larger treed islands, Lantz and Cox, they form the Scott Islands.

A fourth island, Solander, lies off the northwest tip of Brooks Peninsula and its distinguishing features are the same: inaccessibility which provides the birds and mammals with security, and weather so severe that no trees can survive. It is hard to imagine that this fiercely buffeted island is less than 150 miles from the gentle islands of the Gulf of Georgia.

Tufted puffin

Overleaf/

Solander Island, a naturalist's paradise off the northwest coast
161

13/ **The Outer Animals**

A boat rounds the corner and suddenly the air is filled with massive bodies plunging from the high rocks to the safety of the water below. A visit to a colony of Steller's sea lions is always memorable.

Sea lions are massive animals. A mature female may weigh half a ton and bulls several times that, and they make an impressive sight perched on the rocks of some bare offshore islet. In winter there may be 300 or more at each of a dozen spots along Vancouver Island's outer coast, quarrelsome and stinking and growling loud enough to be heard over the roar of the surf. While they spend much of their time stretched out lengthwise like giant slugs, they will be heads up and roaring if anything unusual happens. And if they become at all suspicious of danger, they will be into the water surprisingly quickly, some lumbering laboriously down the rocks, blubber aquiver, others launching themselves into the air from small cliffs. For years, fishermen have been their mortal enemies, and the lions have learned to sense danger.

The best way to see the lions without scaring them into the water is to sneak up on a colony from the rear. The one at Pachena Point is located just a few yards from the forest and a cautious approach can get the viewer just about as close as he cares to be. There is an element of danger, after all: sea lions are carnivores and can inflict nasty wounds. However, the danger of a frontal assault is minimal providing reasonable precautions are taken. The real danger lies in getting in the way of a panicky lion that is trying to escape into the water, and lions jumping off the rocks can easily swamp a small boat. There has been one recorded instance of a fisherman being killed by a lion which landed on top of him, crushing him to death with its weight.

One way to get close to a colony is by small boat, slowly working towards it. Eventually the lions will tolerate the intrusion, and then a subtle change occurs, for while at first the animals seem ready to flee at the slightest false move, they now appear ready to take a stand and

Steller's sea lions gather by the hundreds on the rocks off the west coast

defend their ground against the interloper. The constant rumble of their growls changes from one of fear to one of defiance. Perhaps, put to the test, the big bulls would pull in their fangs and hustle docilely into the ocean, but perhaps not. The rocks belong to these surly and magnificent animals.

Also found in the southern island waters, although mostly in winter, are California sea lions, familiar to many people through their performances at circuses and aquariums. They are darker and smaller than Steller's sea lions, and they bark instead of growl.

The only other similar animals in the waters of Vancouver Island are three species of seals, and all are reasonably easy to recognize. The first, the elephant seal, is the largest seal in the world and also one of the ugliest because of the inflatable snout which gives the species its name. Its center of distribution is in Mexico, but it has been expanding its range in recent years as it has come back from near extinction, and now British Columbia is a regular wintering area for some of the population. Elephant seals never come ashore here but instead float around with only their heads showing above the water. Before the viewer gets his perspective, he may mistake an elephant seal for a sea lion or seal or even a log, but when the size of the creature suddenly becomes evident, there will be no mistaking this monster.

At the other end of the scale is the hair seal, the smallest and most common of the island's seals. While sea lions have been greatly diminished in numbers by control campaigns in past years, the hair seal is still abundant and familiar to anyone who spends time on the coast. Hair seals may be surprised stretched out on rocks below the high tide mark, but more often they are sighted in the water with only their heads visible. If undisturbed, their curiosity may overcome their fear and on occasion, they will follow a boat like a dog.

The third seal found in Vancouver Island waters is the fur seal, an almost legendary species which represents one of the great success stories of conservation, although Vancouver Island receives only the losers. The fur seal is noteworthy for both its rich pelt and its annual lengthy migration from California to Alaska's Pribilof Islands and back again. Alarmed by the fact that uncontrolled slaughter was causing its numbers to dwindle rapidly, the north Pacific nations signed a treaty in 1911 which put it and other marine mammals under rigid control. And the treaty worked, for the fur seal population is now back to full size in the Pribilofs and nearing full size elsewhere.

Because the treaty worked, hundreds of thousands of fur seals now pass by Vancouver Island twice a year, but only those too weak to continue their migration ever land here. And they are generally near death,

The remains of a small whale

pathetic starving little pups which soon succumb — but that is nature's way.

The treaty of 1911 came too late, however, for one of the island's most famous marine mammals, the sea otter. It has the richest fur of any marine mammal in the world and one of the lowest reproductive rates, probably just a single pup every second year. These two factors were enough to give the sea otter the dubious distinction of being the only species of Canadian mammal to become almost extinct as a result of overharvest.

The sea otter closely resembles the common river otter, although there are differences — the former has a shorter tail, larger size and hind flippers very like those of a seal. Its behaviour, however, sets it apart. While both types of otter occur in kelp beds along the west coast, only the sea otter has the habit of lying on its back with a stone balanced on its chest against which it pounds shellfish. This curious behaviour trait qualifies it as one of the very few tool-using mammals and, along with its old-man face, has helped make it one of the most appealing animals on the coast.

Appealing or not, it took the fur exploiters only a hundred years to do the sea otter in. The mandarins of China were willing to pay fabulous prices for its fur at a time when there were no controls, and all along the northwest coast white men traded with Indians for pelts. Vancouver Island became the focus of the slaughter. The exploiters eventually even sold guns to the Indians so that they could hunt the seals more effectively and finally joined in the direct killing themselves, making fortunes while destroying the last of the species on the Canadian coast. Sea otters were given the same protection as fur seals by the treaty of 1911, but it was too late; the species to all intents and purposes was finished. While rumours persisted of occasional sea otters sighted in out-of-the-way spots, they were never confirmed. The sea otter was assumed to be extinct.

Sea otter mother and pup

 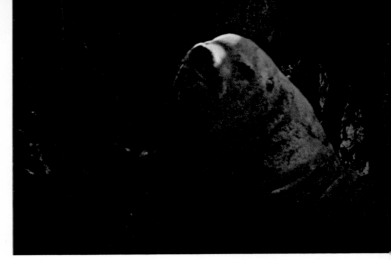

Steller's and California (lower right) sea lions

Occasionally, however, there is an opportunity to undo a mistake, and so it has been with the sea otter. Some had survived and had made a comeback in Alaska and, beginning in 1969, small groups were transplanted to the west coast of Vancouver Island. While they were released at the Bunsby Islands, north of Kyoquot, they apparently soon spread out in all directions, for reports were received of sea otters being sighted at places as far south as Barkley Sound and Race Rocks (near Sooke). This was disappointing, since it was thought that they would do better if they stuck together, but perhaps they are doing all right after all for in the summer of 1971, a sea otter mother and pup were photographed north of Tofino, conclusive proof that the species is reproducing in its new environment. Of course, the new environment is not so different from the old, except perhaps better — more food, a better climate and less competition. With luck, the sea otter will make it and an ecological balance will be restored.

However, less than fifty years after they had destroyed the sea otter, men were at it again off the island's coast, eliminating the whales. Before the coming of the white men, whales of many species were common in the island's waters. Place names still tell the story: Whaletown, Bull Harbor, Blubber Bay, Cachalot Creek. But by the 1960s there was only one whaling station left, Coal Harbor on Holberg Inlet, and it was on the way out because the whales were on their way out. The largest creature that ever lived, the blue whale, has all but disappeared from the waters off Vancouver Island. A few may remain, but it is uncertain whether they can recover, as did the grey whale, or whether they will dwindle to extinction. The Pacific is a big ocean and it is difficult to find mates when numbers are few.

Today the man who sees a large whale must count himself lucky. The most likely to be seen are grey whales since they pass Vancouver Island twice yearly in migrations and feed in close to sandy beaches along the west coast. They may be seen blowing off Long Beach quite regularly and, while most move on by, a few stay off the beach all summer. Grey whales are about forty-five feet long, a far cry from the giant blues which grew to over 100 feet, but they are nevertheless impressive. Watching them roll just beyond the surf, it seems incredible that the Nootka Indians actually hunted them successfully from dugout canoes with mussel-shell harpoons and seal-skin floats.

The sperm, finback, sei, humpback and Pacific right whale were all once common, while a host of smaller whales, dolphins and porpoises still occur along the coast. Probably the best known of these is the killer whale, for years feared as the "wolf of the sea." It is an appellation that was probably more accurate than people realized, for after aquariums began catching killer whales, it was found that they were gentle and inteligent, much, in fact, like wolves. But while they can be trained to do impressive tricks in a pool, they are much more awesome rolling through wild seas, the shiny black dorsal fins of the bulls projecting eight feet high as they shepherd the cows and calves. Unfortunately, there are suspicions that killer whales too are declining, although no one can be certain since acceptable records have only recently begun to be kept.

While the size of the porpoises is much less impressive, their antics are memorable for those people lucky enough to encounter them. They will sometimes ride on the bow wave of a boat, seemingly testing their swimming skills against the speed of the machine and will accompany one for miles, darting swiftly back and forth in front of it.

Besides true marine mammals, there are many other animals along the island's shoreline. Racoons may often be seen ambling along a beach or mudflat, while a mink may be spotted dragging its young by the scruff of the neck from one shelter to another, or a family of river otters may be sighted racing into the water. Occasionally on an isolated beach, one of the more secretive species such as a marten may be glimpsed. Both

Cormorants nesting in the eroded cliffs of Gabriola Island

black bears and the ubiquitous deer do well near the coast, too — the bear because of the abundance of food and the deer because of the mildness of the winters. Deer will frequently be seen swimming considerable distances in the ocean and sometimes may even be observed eating kelp and other seaweed, perhaps for the salt or for the algae which is reasonably nutritious. Deer are often hard-pressed to find a hearty meal in winter. Where there are deer, there are also cougars and wolves, but while their tracks may be visible, the animals themselves are rarely sighted.

For every mammalian species that frequents the island's shores, there seem to be half a dozen types of birds, and every coastal naturalist should make a trip to a seabird nesting colony.

There are at least three major types of bird colonies, two of them readily accessible. But this easy access, if abused, can result in the colony's destruction for nesting seabirds cannot tolerate much disturbance. If they are kept off their nests too long during incubation, the unhatched chicks can die of heat or cold as can hatched chicks too young to leave the nest. The danger is even greater when the chicks become mobile, for they are safe only within the immediate vicinity of the nest; the moment they leave, they are in danger of being mercilessly attacked as intruders invading the territory of their neighbours. At this crucial stage, a dog running through the bird colony or even a man walking can result in losses of up to ninety per cent of the young, and it does not take long for the colony to become deserted.

Cormorant chick

There are places where nesting seabirds can be observed with less fear of disturbance. One such place is Mitlenatch Island, a provincial park north of Courtenay and a typical nesting area for gulls and cormorants. These species are commonly found on rocky, grass-covered islets far enough from land that predators cannot easily reach them by swimming, and Mitlenach qualifies since it lies in the middle of the Strait of Georgia.

A colony such as this one clearly illustrates the different problems facing seabirds and terrestrial species. Terrestrial birds must usually defend a large enough territory to provide them with food; seabirds find food less of a problem but must find a predation-free nest site and crowd as many birds as possible into it. Thus gulls and cormorants defend just enough territory to provide them with a suitable nest site which may mean only the area within beak range when the bird is sitting on its nest. The competition for such space is intense, and the adult gulls can be observed on their territories in early February despite the fact that eggs may not be laid until the early summer. Once a bird has possession of a piece of ground, it has the advantage and will usually emerge the winner in any territorial dispute.

On an island such as Mitlenatch, the birds generally arrange themselves so that the gulls have the flatter ground while the cormorants take over steeper rock faces near the edge of the water, building bulky nests practically one on top of the other. By mid-summer, the colony resembles an apartment complex.

But there will still be some room left for species such as the pigeon guillemots which nest in crevices in the rock or oyster-catchers which drop their eggs in small depressions on bare stone loosely lined with bits of clam shell.

Oyster-catchers are striking black birds about the size of crows with bright red bills for probing among the rocks and the typical stilt legs of a shorebird. Pigeon guillemots are also black with red feet and bills, but their bills are short, they have webbed feet like a duck and white wing patches. The bird they most closely resemble is the penguin, and they inhabit a somewhat similar niche in the environment since they are true seabirds, members of a group known as alcids. Alcids are fish-eaters, and most of the group nest in burrows, making the pigeon guillemot something of an exception in a group that includes murres, murrelets, auklets and puffins.

A second type of seabird colony is the most spectacular and the one which can be viewed with the least danger to the birds since it occurs on a cliff face. The island's best example is the one on Gabriola Island. Cormorants are ideally suited to such a cliff face existence, but other species can be found here as well.

The third type of colony, where seabirds nest in holes in the ground, as at Triangle Island, is always difficult of access. Here are found puffins, recognizable by their parrot-like beaks, and rhinoceros auklets, a duller species with a thinner beak, named for the curious orange projection that grows off the top of their beaks during the breeding season, probably for the purpose of attracting a mate. The burrows in such alcid colonies are also used by petrels, small birds with the delicate appearance of songbirds but possessing webbed feet and elongated wings to enable them to soar over the ocean.

Vancouver Island also has a mystery seabird, the marbled murrelet. This small mottled alcid is common around the island and obviously nests nearby, but amateur and professional biologists had looked for their nests for years without notable success until recently when two chicks dropped out of a tree which a logger was felling near Holberg. It is therefore possible that marbled murrelets nest in holes in trees like a few species of ducks.

It is the waterfowl which make the most use of Vancouver Island's coastline. A major wintering area for ducks, geese and trumpeter swans,

Rhinoceros auklet

Many small islands serve as nesting colonies for gulls and cormorants

Sandpiper

the coast also serves as a resting and feeding area for hundreds of thousands of additional waterbirds during spring and fall migration. Mallards and scaup settle into the island's estuaries for weeks at a time, particularly along the west coast, but the spring brant migration attracts the most interest. The brant travel from Mexico by the tens of thousands to settle along the beaches of the southeast coast from mid-March until mid-May, and they are everywhere, feeding on eel-grass before they lift off again for their breeding grounds in Alaska.

And of course the island's shores are replete with other species — small birds like killdeers and sandpipers, large ones like bald eagles and ospreys. One of the most striking is the great blue heron, a tall crane-like species which will stand patiently for hours waiting for a fish to come within range of its spear-like bill. Crows and ravens are prominent, and crows in particular forage along the shore in great numbers.

No account of the island's coastal wildlife would be complete without mention of the fish. Salmon have made Vancouver Island famous, particularly among sports fishermen, but other species abound. There are smelt, small sardine-like fish of at least six different types which arrive at the island's beaches each fall to spawn. They lie massed offshore until the tide is right and then hurl themselves onto the beach to lay their eggs in the sand along the high-tide line, so numerous that a person can literally scoop them out of the water by the bucketful.

A feast like this does not go unattended: the gulls and dogfish get their fill. The dogfish, small sharks about three feet long, will follow the smelts practically onto the beach, feeding so close to shore that their dorsal fins are out of the water and the sound of their teeth is clearly audible. It is not unusual for dogfish to group together and even when no major fish run is present, giant schools of them may be encountered, especially visible at night when their eyes reflect light as do those of a cat.

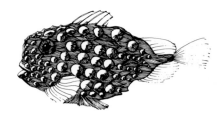

Spiny lumpsucker

While dogfish are the island's most common shark, they are dwarfed by the larger species. The largest of all is the basking shark which from above looks something like a submarine since a good-sized specimen will run to forty or fifty feet. It poses no significant danger, eating only plankton, but it is not popular with fishermen because of its propensity for getting wrapped up in their nets. This problem has caused the species to be persecuted as relentlessly as the sea lion, and, like the sea lion, it has declined in recent years. The island will be a poorer place if it disappears.

There are also the unexpected specimens — the rock-boring clams and the tuna that turn up off the west coast every so often and the giant leatherback turtles which appear even less frequently at unlikely spots like Nootka and Quatsino Sound.

Fishermen claim you never know what sort of sea creature will be encountered next; it is a big ocean, incredibly diverse and full of surprises. The same could be said of Vancouver Island as a whole. Nobody could ever know it all, but it is a place that invites the attempt.

The Bunsby Islands at dawn